Say Yes!

Rick Wakeman

Hodder & Stoughton
LONDON SYDNEY AUCKLAND

This book is dedicated to just four
of the many people who have touched
my life:
Mildred Wakeman, who brought me to life,
Cyril Wakeman, who shaped my life,
Nina Wakeman, my partner in life,
and
Jesus, who gave me life

British Library Cataloguing in Publication Data
A record for this book is available from the British Library

ISBN 0 340 62151 6

Typeset by Hewer Text Composition Services, Edinburgh
Printed and bound in Great Britain by
Cox & Wyman, Reading, Berks.

Hodder and Stoughton Ltd
A division of Hodder Headline PLC
338 Euston Road
London NW1 3BH

Preface

Write an autobiography? Surely the easiest thing to do in the world? After all, all you basically have to do is put into words some of the more important events that have mapped out your life. However, it's not until you actually start writing down these "more important events" that you realise exactly what has been responsible for shaping your existence on this earth.

More often than not, you discover that it was the most unlikely elements that were responsible for the major changes that have taken place. I found that what I previously thought to be important in my life was constantly being proved wrong. Amazingly it was the irrelevancies that showed themselves to be the real importances. On completion of the book, it was in fact quite an eye-opener to read it back to myself and really discover how and why I am what I am now.

People say that the funniest stories are those of real life and that's certainly been true as far as I have been concerned. However, I had no idea that I had really experienced sadness, either, or of the amazing amount of mistakes I had made.

In reality, the most bizarre events, unlikely people and strange places were what was responsible for the shaping of my life. For example, who would have thought that the social club for the mentally retarded at Neasden would have merited even a mention in a book such as this?

The truth is that my life has been extremely anecdotal. Link the relevant anecdotes together, and in a nutshell you have my life. With Christianity as the true catalyst, I now have a chance for my life to become a meaningful one. Writing this book has been an important step in this never-ending process.

Contents

1

In the beginning was the piano

It's amazing the things you remember as a small child. Believe it or not, I can remember crawling. Unable to propel myself in a forward direction, I used to crawl backwards and get jammed under the sideboard in the dining room of my parents' small semi-detached house in north London.

Then I would scream.

I can vividly remember getting my first tricycle. I can also vividly remember falling off my first tricycle. I really loved that bike. My father, Cyril Frank Wakeman, unable to afford a new one, had bought it second hand, dismantled it and repainted the frame before oiling and greasing all the moving parts, finally putting it back together in time for Father Christmas to bring it to me in 1953.

Like all small children I loved Father Christmas and really believed in him. I did in fact believe in two people I had never seen – Father Christmas and God. At the age of seven, Father Christmas was crossed off the list. That left God.

Two years prior to Father Christmas's sad demise, I had started day school at Wood End Infants in Northolt, Middlesex. About the same time I also started Sunday School at South Harrow Baptist Church. I loved them both, but I liked Sunday School better as you didn't get the slipper or get rapped over the knuckles with a ruler when you misbehaved. It followed, therefore, that you misbehaved considerably more on a Sunday.

My family were what I would describe as a respectfully Christian one. My father was a deacon at West End Baptist Church in London, his father was a Baptist lay preacher and my mother, Mildred, although raised a Methodist, attended the same church as me.

Sundays were very special days. My mother and I would walk about a mile and a half to South Harrow Baptist Church for the morning service and Sunday School and my father would go off to his church in Hammersmith, where he had belonged nearly all his life; and that I suppose is the key to a strong relationship with a church, a sense of belonging.

Sundays were also my introduction to comedy. After *The Billy Cotton Band Show*, on the BBC's now sadly-departed Light Programme, came to an end with the strains of "Somebody Stole My Girl" and "Legion Patrol", the radio turned its attention to such masterpieces as *The Navy Lark*, *The Clitheroe Kid*, *Round the Horne* and *Beyond Our Ken*. I formed an instant empathy with the Kenneth Williams, Kenneth Hornes and Bill Pertwees of this world which remains with me to this very day.

We didn't have our first television until 1956 and so, until the square box "took over", musical evenings completed Sundays. My father's brother, Stan, would bring his ukelele and join my father on the piano, with my mother adding what could be dubiously classed as "vocals". In later years my cousin Alan joined in on clarinet and saxophone and his brother Keith produced a violin. I think it was a combination of the violin and my mother's rendition of "Nellie Dean" that marked the death knell for the musical evenings and the appearance of a For Sale sign outside next-door's house.

I was fascinated by these musical soirées and after being put to bed used to get up, sneak downstairs and listen at the door to the front room where it all took place, so when my father told me I had been accepted for piano lessons with the very highly rated Mrs Dorothy Symes, I was over the moon.

Here was the first stage on my road to stardom. Not *Sunday Night at the London Palladium*, but Sunday night in the front room of 19 Wood End Gardens in Northolt, Middlesex.

I remember my very first lesson. I was really excited, but very frightened. I was just six. I hung my coat up in the little annexe and walked through the door into the music teaching room where Mrs Symes sat waiting.

"Hello, Richard," she said.

"Hello, Mrs Symes."

Not the most riveting of conversations, I admit, but all relationships have to start somewhere.

Over the next fifteen years, Mrs Symes was to become the most important person in my life outside my parents. She possessed patience as well as a wonderful ability to teach music. She actually needed more of the former ability as far as I was concerned as, looking back and being totally honest, I must have been an absolute nightmare.

Initially all went well. I loved to practise and leapt forward very quickly. After just a few weeks I had booked myself in for the Sunday musical evenings and made my debut with an eleven-second rendition of "Buy a Broom", which was met with moderate indifference as my mother was in the kitchen making the tea, Uncle Stan was tuning his ukelele and my father was sorting out some music, but nevertheless I went to bed happy and convinced of my future career. I was going to be a musician, a concert pianist or maybe a conductor.

Lessons continued and I was entered for my first festival: the Southall Music Festival, to be exact. I nervously arrived with Mrs Symes and my parents, having prepared the set piece. Thirty other hopefuls sat in the hall, whilst the adjudicator had to sit through a variety of performances of the same piece, ranging from musical to diabolical. (I can remember mentally crossing off adjudicator as part of my future musical career.)

An hour later and we had all played. An exhausted adjudicator staggered to the front. He mumbled on about timing and fingering and practice, etc., and then announced the marks.

"Number one . . . Janet Williams, seventy-eight marks; number two . . . Barry Hyams, eighty-two marks; number three . . ." and so it went on. I waited patiently for my number, twenty-two.

"Number twenty-one . . . Marjory Thomson, eighty-three marks; number twenty-three . . . John Davidson, seventy-nine marks."

I was really confused. I turned to Mrs Symes and started to mouth, "He's missed me out," but Mrs Symes just smiled and motioned to me to sit still and keep quiet.

"Number twenty-two, Richard Wakeman."

I sat bolt upright, terrified and convinced he was going to tear me apart. After all, why else would he leave me out of the marking?

"A wonderfully musical all-round performance for one so young."

(I was ten.)

"He is my clear winner with eighty-eight marks."

Mrs Symes and my parents beamed. I was dumbstruck.

"He'll get his trophy at the prizewinners' concert in a few weeks' time," said Mrs Symes.

For the next ten months, things went uphill at a phenomenal rate of knots. I entered festival after festival and kept on winning. I really felt unassailable and Jack the Lad.

Then the bubble burst.

Wimbledon Music Festival.

I came third.

I cried.

I threw a tantrum that would put McEnroe to shame. I was inconsolable.

I can recall overhearing Mrs Symes talking to my father.

"Thank heavens for that. I have been worried ever since he won his first festival. I really thought he would have lost one by now, but unfortunately after such a long time he thinks he has a divine right to win everything and that just isn't so. I have actually started entering him for harder festival classes in older age groups which should help to bring him back down to earth, so don't worry, he'll get over it."

He didn't.

I like winning.

I practised even harder and although I didn't win everything that moved, I certainly won more than my fair share. It was a real mixture of emotions, I suppose. I loved an audience to play in front of and I loved the piano.

Things were to move sideways, though, as I entered my teens. Other influences started to enter my life. Football and cricket were two important areas which ate into piano practice time, as was the ever-increasing attraction of the opposite sex.

Piano practice suffered, and Mrs Symes must have had sleepless nights over my diversionary interests which clearly slowed down my progress.

She made it very clear to me that if I was to achieve my aim and get into the Royal College of Music then I would have to knuckle down and work much harder, as I was falling behind in the schedule of graded examinations, both in the playing and in theory.

(This is now an opportune moment to confess for the first time the whereabouts of over a hundred rubber erasers, whose mysterious disappearance from the theory classes over a period of about four years completely baffled Mrs Symes. Malcolm Ball and I used to stuff as many rubbers as possible into our pockets after the classes, and then sit on the bridge by Sudbury Hill railway station and attempt to drop them into the funnels of passing steam engines before the smoke forced us to jump off the bridge, spluttering and coughing.)

Mrs Symes made an impassioned plea to my father. "He's wasting your money and my time. It's a great shame because he has the natural talent to go far."

I never realised until much later how clever my father was at handling the situation. Very casually he said to me, "I

know you've got a lot on your plate at the moment with your
football in the winter, your cricket in the summer, the youth
club down the church and the Boys' Brigade, so you might as
well knock the piano on the head. You're not doing enough
practice and Mrs Symes says it's a waste of time. Shame,
really, as she says you have a talent, but let me know when
you want to pack it in and I'll give her a ring."

That was it.

I had expected the reading of the riot act about how I had
to knuckle down, etc., but my father had basically said he
couldn't care less and nor did anyone else, and therein lay
the clever catalyst that threw me into overdrive.

After self-analysis I realised that I had a difficult task in
front of me. I was behind at school, where I needed at least
two A-levels to accompany my application to the Royal
College of Music, plus I needed a distinction at the final
piano grade and also had to reach a reasonable standard on
my second instrument, which was the clarinet.

I knuckled down as best I could and from the age of
seventeen gave it my best shot.

The A-levels were a problem. I was taking three: Music,
Art and British Constitution (Politics).

Music should have been easy except for the fact that it
was in three parts: Theory (no problem), Aural (no problem)
and Music History (big problem). I had not studied the
pieces properly or studied the musical periods set out in
the syllabus.

My music master, William Herrera, was convinced I would
fail this section, which would mean I would fail the whole
examination as you had to get at least a pass in each part.
We had a blazing row about three weeks before the exam
where he said I had wasted his time and everybody else's
time and that I wouldn't pass even if I was given all the
answers.

He was right, of course, but I argued with him and it
culminated with him betting me ten shillings (50p) that I
wouldn't pass.

Ten shillings was a small fortune to me back in the late sixties and worth about ten pounds today.

I worked night and day trying to cram two years' work into three weeks.

I then sweated whilst waiting for the results. I knew it could go either way.

And Bill Herrera?

Bill, who was in his late fifties, eventually ran off with a fifth-form girl to Spain where they married and lived for the next ten years before he died. Many who knew him believe his death was a combination of exasperation, caused by me, and exhaustion, caused by his young wife!

The second A-level I took was British Constitution. We were warned by the teacher that all the papers were liable to be marked by professors who had serious left-wing tendencies and so to be careful how we approached the questions which allowed for viewpoints.

I've always had this rebellious streak in me, and to this day I don't know why I did it, but I basically wrote answers that would suit a manifesto for the far right of the Conservative party. I knew I'd failed the moment I put my pen down, but I had a broad grin on my face.

Just Art to go. The examination was also in sections, and the final part was to produce an abstract painting with the title "Fugue".

I had three hours.

After two and a half hours I had a waste-paper bin full of rejected ideas. It was a nightmare.

With fifteen minutes to go I was desperate. I pinned a fresh piece of paper to a board and propped it up against a wall.

I threw paint at it which ran in dribbles down the paper. I threw ink at it. I threw sawdust at it. I threw anything I could find at it, and then with ten minutes left I hastily drew in as many musical symbols as I could squeeze in, using coloured ink. I recall the art master, Mike Westbrook, looking in total disbelief at what I had produced. I attached my details to the finished product and went home, via the pub.

I drowned my sorrows quite severely. I knew it was all going to end in tears. I had worked really hard for the last few weeks, but deep down I knew that I had left it too late. On top of my A-levels I had had to prepare for my final grade at the piano, practise the clarinet, do the final grade at music theory and also sit my entrance examination for the Royal College of Music.

Couple with this the fact that I was also working in the evenings as a piano player in local pubs and working men's clubs, and you can see where my despondency was coming from.

The day of my entrance exam for the Royal College of Music arrived with my waking up with an unbelievable bout of flu. I was coughing and spluttering badly, but with my music under one arm and my clarinet in the other, I set off for Prince Consort Road behind the Royal Albert Hall where the imposing building of the Royal College of Music awaited my arrival.

The piano-performing side of things went very well and I knew I had impressed. The theory also went well, as strangely enough did the history paper. The clarinet I knew was going to be a stumbling block. I had decided that I no longer really liked the clarinet – I think Acker Bilk's "Stranger on the Shore" had a lot to do with it – and so I really hadn't practised. My standard was nowhere near that which was required and I knew it would let me down and probably cost me the offer of a place.

I approached the room for my clarinet "interview" with trepidation, a runny nose and a cough.

A curt "Enter" answered my knock.

Three men sat behind a desk. A single chair and a music stand made up the furniture.

"Now you are Mr Wakeman, is that correct?"

"Yes," I spluttered, accompanied by sneezes, coughs and a nose blow which sounded like the "Trumpet Voluntary".

"Are you feeling OK?" one of them asked.

"Not really, sir," I replied, "I'm full of flu."

"Well, in that case you're in no fit state to blow a clarinet, so just sit down and we'll ask you some questions about your playing and I think that will suffice."

I gratefully sat down.

"How would you describe your tonal quality on the clarinet?" the professor in the centre enquired.

"Dreadful," I answered truthfully.

They chuckled.

"Do you know the Weber concertino?"

"Yes. I can't play it, but I know it."

They chuckled again.

"Would you say you were of orchestral standard?"

"Yes sir. School orchestra standard."

Guffaws.

"Well, thank you, Mr Wakeman, that will be all."

I sat on the Piccadilly Line underground train on the way home with mixed feelings. Perhaps I had been too honest as regards the clarinet, it would surely let me down. I felt confident I had done well in all the other areas; I could have kicked myself.

Shortly before I sat my first A-level, a letter arrived from the Royal College. They were offering me a place subject to my gaining the necessary two A-levels and passing my grade eight exams.

I couldn't believe it. I could only think that they had offered the place to me on the strength of my piano playing and had made special allowances as regards my obvious deficiency with the clarinet.

I passed both the necessary grade eight exams and so now everything hinged on how I had done with my A-levels.

I really thought I had little chance. I had made a serious effort as regards the music history but felt deep down that I hadn't done quite enough to get through. British Constitution was a lost cause, and as for Art – well, let's face it, better graffiti has been seen on public-toilet walls.

In August the post office delivered thousands of letters containing examination results to students' homes all over the country. I stared at the brown envelope that lay on the mat for what seemed an eternity. My parents were both at work.

I eventually picked it up and sat down in the tiny kitchen with the envelope staring up at me from the table.

I opened it and removed the small piece of paper that over the decades has both created and destroyed careers.

In the sixties, marking was as follows: A, B, C, D, and E were passes, O was considered as an O-level pass on an A-level paper, and F was a failure.

On the top of the slip were my name and the name of my school, Drayton Manor County Grammar School. Then it just gave the A-level results:

British Constitution F (no surprise there)
Music E

I couldn't believe it. I'd passed. Against all odds. I remember my heart beating loud and fast. I looked away from the slip in total bemusement and then looked back for the final result.

Art C

C! Who on earth had marked it, Picasso's brother? Who cares? I was ecstatic. I phoned both my mother and my father at their respective workplaces, and also Mrs Symes. Two days later an envelope dropped through the letter-box with a crisp ten-shilling note in it and a letter which said.

Dear Richard,
Never in my whole life have I been so happy to hand over ten shillings. Hopefully you realise how hard you made it for yourself and this situation will never again arise in your life.
Best wishes,
                              Bill Herrera
I wish to this day I had kept the letter.

*   *   *

My first week at college was hilarious to say the least. I knew things were going to be tough as since I was living at home my grant was a mere thirty-seven pounds, which wasn't even enough to cover the cost of the necessary books I had to buy. Once again my father came to the rescue, and like most teenagers I failed at the time to realise the sacrifices he made in order for me to pursue my musical education.

The first day of term arrived and I went to the main hall for the welcoming assembly. The guest speaker was an "old boy", Yehudi Menuhin.

He was introduced by Sir Keith Faulkner, the principal. The great man walked on to the platform, turned and faced the gathered throng, and stood on his head.

He remained in this position for about fifteen minutes. Not a word was spoken. The odd titter from the students was met with disapproving glances. Finally he reversed the process and standing on two feet gave a twenty-minute lecture on yoga.

I have been concerned for his mental health ever since.

Next in line was to collect a list of our allotted professors from the men's counsellor, Mr Gillett, and then visit each professor individually and work out a schedule with them as to when our individual lessons would take place.

I was dearly hoping I would get Antony Hopkins as my piano professor but I had no such luck. I had been allotted a Rhodesian lady by the name of Eileen Reynolds, whom I went along to see in her tuition room.

She did not like me and I did not like her style of teaching at all. She was not a bit like Mrs Symes in either attitude or understanding. A bond of hatred grew extremely quickly. I knew I would never pass my mid-term exams with Mrs Reynolds and so unbeknown to the college I returned privately to Mrs Symes, who coached me through with flying colours.

Mrs Reynolds does have one claim to fame, though, as far as I am concerned. It concerns a note in my pigeon-hole which appeared one morning asking me to visit the men's counsellor, Mr Gillett.

After a few pleasantries he said to me, "Your fur."

"My what?" I replied.

"Your fur," he repeated, touching his hair. "Mrs Reynolds has met with me and says she doesn't like it. It's too long and she wants it cut."

"Cow" was the first word that sprang to mind, but thankfully it never reached my lips. My hair actually did not even touch my collar and I had never ever had it long at all; strangely enough, that very day I had also planned to have it cut, but this ludicrous meeting with Mr Gillett infuriated me.

"Mr Gillett. With all due respect I fail to see how on earth my appearance affects my performance here at the college. I have passed all my mid-term exams with very high grades and have not missed one lecture. I have also enrolled for additional tuition in modern music and orchestration and have worked really hard. Also it may interest you to know that I had every intention of having my hair cut this afternoon after the art of music lecture with Antony Hopkins."

"Well, that solves the problem, then."

"No it doesn't, Mr Gillett. You can relay the message back to Mrs Reynolds that I will not be having my hair cut this afternoon."

"When will you be having it cut, then?"

"I won't."

And I didn't.

Not for five years.

Thank you, Mrs Reynolds.

My clarinet teacher was Basil Tchaikof. I was stunned. He was a famous professor and normally only took the very advanced and brilliant clarinet pupils.

Why me?

I approached his room cautiously and entered on his beckoning.

"Come in, Mr Wakeman. How nice to see you."

Basil Tchaikof was a lovely warm man who was obviously pleased to see me.

I relaxed.

"I am so pleased to have you as a pupil," he said.

"Normally I don't take second-study pupils, but your report was so excellent I felt obliged to take you on."

I unrelaxed.

"Pardon?"

"It says on my report that you were unable to actually play at the entrance examination but that you are obviously a very advanced and skilful player. It also says you are clearly very modest and have a pleasant, amusing streak to your nature."

He won't find it funny in a minute, I thought to myself. Thinking back to the examining room it now became clear what had happened: my honesty they had misread as modesty, and with the other areas of my entrance examination being of a high standard had obviously classed my clarinet playing in the same ilk.

I did my very best to clarify all of this to Basil Tchaikof and the colour slowly drained from his face. He lost a lot of that warm, friendly glow that had been so apparent when I had entered the room.

"Surely you can't be that appalling?" he asked hopefully.

I slowly nodded.

Still somewhat disbelieving he made an appointment with me for two days' time for my first lesson.

Those were two of the longest days of my life.

During the first few days at the Royal College I had struck up a friendship with another student, John McDermot, who hailed from Darwen in Lancashire. His first study was flute, but more importantly, his father was the senior rep for Thwaites' Brewery. I spent many a happy day with John and his father touring the working men's clubs during the summer. Thwaites had this lethal drink called Old Tom. I became very fond of Old Tom.

The college had ninety-eight practice rooms, each equipped

with a piano, music stands, etc., for students to practise during the day when not at lectures or having private tuition. There was a pub just around the corner, called the Queen's Arms, which was the college "local". For obvious reasons, this particular hostelry was known as the "Ninety-nine" in which John and I spent many hours "practising".

And so came the day of my first clarinet lesson with Basil Tchaikof.

In the two days leading up to my own personal Armageddon I had really put in some serious practice on the instrument, but it has to be said that little progress was made. I had never ever practised for more than half an hour a day on the clarinet before, and so eight hours in two days swelled my lips up to Al Jolson proportions, and to say they were sore would be putting it politely.

I sat in the college canteen gazing into my coffee, which stung the moment I put it to my lips.

John joined me.

"You been in a fight, Rick?"

"Eh?"

"Your mouth looks like it's taken a severe pasting."

"It has, I've been practising the clarinet. I've got Basil Tchaikof this afternoon, remember."

I had taken John into my confidence over the clarinet situation, and after he had got over his initial amusement he had shown considerable sympathy for my plight.

"You need a drink," he said.

"That's the last thing I need."

"Look, Rick, you're tense and on top of that your mouth is really sore. A drop of Scotch will help your lips and relax you at the same time. Come on, it's ten thirty, they'll just have opened."

I must admit I did feel better after the first Scotch. I felt even better after the fifth and absolutely tremendous after the tenth.

"What's the time?" I mumbled.

"A quarter to two," came the slurred reply from John, who

seemed to have lost total interest in my upcoming problem and was chatting up two attractive female sopranos who had popped in for lunch.

"What!"

"A quarter to two. What time's your lesson?"

"Two o'clock!"

There was more than a hint of panic in the voice as I grabbed my clarinet case, ran out of the Ninety-nine and headed towards the college.

It has to be said that I was relaxed. Relaxed as a newt, to be precise. I staggered up the steps of the college and looked on the board to see which room Basil Tchaikof was teaching in that day. Just my luck, he was right at the top of the building and there was no lift.

I ran up the stairs, and by the time I reached the top I felt very, very dizzy and could hardly stand. I also felt sick, and realising that I stank of whisky contemplated turning around and sending a message that I was ill, but for some inexplicable reason I found myself gaping through the glass in the door like some demented animal in a zoo.

Basil Tchaikof saw this apparition and nearly jumped out of his skin. Quickly calming down, he motioned to me to come in.

I turned the door handle and it just went round and round. He motioned again for me to enter.

I tried pushing the door.

Nothing.

Basil Tchaikof just stared back in amazement as I took four paces back and commenced preparation for a shoulder charge.

He stepped forward and opened the door from his side.

"You have to push the handle first and then turn it," he said.

I walked in. It was worse than the dentist. It seemed worse than anything at the time.

It's funny how the mind works when you're drunk. For starters you are always convinced that nobody notices that you've had too much and that you can bluff your way through anything.

In retrospect, I can honestly say that Basil had spotted my problem.

However, at the time I had not spotted that Basil had spotted my problem and so the charade began.

I stood in the middle of the room, grinning in a manner intended to ooze confidence. I must have looked like a demented Cheshire cat.

"I think we may find it easier to start the lesson if you take the clarinet out of its case, Mr Wakeman."

Blast. Slipped up there. Nevertheless, I was still convinced that he was not aware that he was about to teach a student containing most of the Queen's Arms' Scotch.

After several attempts to fit the component parts of the clarinet together, accompanied by grunts, groans, hiccups and stupid mutterings such as, "I'm sure this bit fits in there, no, in there, well perhaps it's this bit," Basil walked over, and taking the three parts fitted them together.

"Brilliant," I said.

"Pardon?"

"I'm a little nervous, Mr Tchaikof." I was aware that my speech was slurring, but I determined to soldier on.

"Let's start with a scale. G, two octaves."

I placed the clarinet to my lips. The reed caught on my top teeth and snapped at the end.

"I've broken my reed, Mr Tchaikof."

"So you have. I'm sure you have a spare reed, so change it as quickly as you can."

This, I felt, was fate lending me a hand. I must surely have already used up half of my allotted half-hour lesson. A reed change could use up another few minutes, a couple of quick scales and it could be all over. Great. I started to brighten up.

After several abortive attempts at changing the reed, Basil came over and did it for me.

"Brilliant," I said.

"Pardon?"

"I'm a little nervous."

(Why do drunks keep repeating themselves?)

"Scale of G, Mr Wakeman."

Mr Wakeman played three notes and passed out.

I opened my eyes and tried to work out where I was. My head ached, I felt sick and I could hear music.

I was lying on the sofa in the teaching room and a girl was playing the clarinet with Basil Tchaikof standing by the side of her.

"Yes, that's good, Fiona. Just watch the runs over the break."

He heard me groan.

"Ah. Mr Wakeman seems to have returned to the land of the living. You may leave us, Fiona." Fiona left.

"Get up."

I tried.

"*Get up*."

I realised that I was on sticky ground.

"You're paralytic."

Very sticky ground.

I stood up and prepared myself for the onslaught that was to follow.

And it did.

It was full of the obvious and, it has to be said, well deserved. Lots of "disgracefuls" and "abuse of privileges" and "a full report to the principal" were littered throughout the next five or so minutes.

Then he told me to sit down.

I thought I saw a glimmer of a smile cross his face.

I told him exactly what had happened and why.

"It happened to me once, you know," he said.

I looked at him in stunned amazement.

"I was playing in an orchestra for a ballet at a theatre. The clarinets had nothing to do for about fifteen minutes in one section, and so we used to sneak out of the pit and go over the road to the pub for a swift couple of drinks and

then sneak back in time for the next time we had to play.
Well, on this particular occasion we hadn't had anything to
eat and the rush back to the theatre really hit us, and as I
tried to quietly retake my place I fell over and knocked a
couple of music stands over, which then proceeded to knock
the ones in front of them over like a house of cards. It was
chaos."

He smiled at the memory.

"You don't like the clarinet very much, do you?"

"I do, actually," I said truthfully. "It's just that I'm no
good at it."

"Well, we're going to have to get you through the mid-term
exam somehow. What do you think?"

"I'll do my very best, sir," I replied.

And I did, and I passed the mid-term exam and he never
mentioned the incident again. Well, not in my presence
anyway!

I left the room and there at the top of the stairs to meet
me was John McDermot, who had a big grin on his face.
Fiona was standing next to him.

"It went rather well," I said, and fell down the stairs.

2

Band of hope

For as long as I can remember I always wanted to be a musician of one sort or another. I vaguely recall the odd fleeting diversionary ambitions which included becoming a policeman and joining the army, but such admirable careers never really threatened the burning desire to make music publicly.

Strangely enough, the record that probably subconsciously inspired my interest in pop music was "Say I won't be there" by the Springfields.

I was intrigued by the acoustic guitar which in one section had a guitar-string bending which created an out-of-tune effect with the "third" of the chord. In effect I had been introduced to the "blue" note. I can remember rushing to the piano to find this mythical note. I discovered where it was but couldn't play it as it appeared to be down the crack between the keys.

I was probably about twelve or thirteen at the time, and up until this moment my progress along the pop/rock route had been pretty uneventful. A year of playing Russ Conway's "Side Saddle" had not done much for me and I was not getting a great deal of progressive satisfaction out of the traditional jazz band that I was in at school. Suddenly I had found something that genuinely excited and frustrated me.

I was excited by the sound of this blue note and frustrated because I couldn't play it!

Armed with four or five weeks' pocket-money, I set off for the local record shop. The experiments with Rothman's King Size were about to be replaced with a blues album on the Pye Golden Guinea label.

I ran home as fast as I could, realising almost immediately that if I had spent more of my pocket-money on records and less on cigarettes I would have been able to run home much faster.

Switching on my Dansette Major record-player, I waited eagerly for the somewhat worn stylus to hit the groove. I vividly recall the first couple of tracks boring me rigid. Then, just as I was calculating the disc's second-hand value, on it came. I hastily picked up the cover to see what this wondrous track was, and there in bold print was stage two in my new-found musical education: "Rinky Dink" by Dave "Baby" Cortez.

More experiments followed on the piano and I discovered quite quickly how to create a false blue note on the keyboard. I was so excited by this that everything I now played had a blue note in it somewhere – well actually everywhere, to be more precise.

Mrs Symes, my long-suffering piano teacher, was not impressed with my inclusion of blue notes in Haydn sonatas and Bach preludes and fugues, and was also unable to explain to me why Haydn and Bach had never written any pieces with them in in the first place.

I was genuinely very excited. I started buying any record I could which had an organ or piano on it, and literally every single one disappointed me. Trad jazz was very popular at that time, 1963, the three "B"s being the most popular artists: Kenny Ball, Acker Bilk and Chris Barber. I was the co-founder of the school trad jazz band which we called Brother Wakeman and the Clergymen. Every band had a uniform at that time; as schoolboys we couldn't afford anything like that and so we came up with the idea of turning our shirts round, creating the dog-collar effect, and then buttoning up our blazers from behind. The band was actually quite popular and we performed at quite a few school concerts.

However, after discovering my new-found influences, I very much wanted to introduce them into the band. My cousin, Alan Wakeman, who was and still is a superb clarinettist and saxophone player, was moving very much down the modern jazz route and was also influencing the band in that direction. This was tricky for me as I hated modern jazz (and still do). Alan and I, though, were always great friends and were eventually musically united through the realisation that "Playing what the heart desires does not feed what the stomach requires"!

But at the tender age of fourteen the heart could rule, and so I started hanging around youth clubs where bands were playing. They were all pretty dreadful but at the time they all had an incredible magnetic attraction. Very few of them had a pianist or organist. There were very logical reasons for this, of course, as there were only two types of organ worth having, the Hammond being the Rolls-Royce model and the Vox Continental being a sort of mid-range Ford Granada.

I realised that in order to get into a band I had to have my own organ. I could in no way afford either of the aforementioned marques and so set my sights on what Woolworth's had to offer, which was a mini-keyed reed model which sounded like a mouth organ and had about as much impact within a band as a dachshund would in the Grand National. Nevertheless it was all that I could financially set my sights on, as the smallest Hammond was a thousand pounds and a Vox Continental was over six hundred. The Woolworth Super Deluxe Reed Organ was twenty-three pounds. This also included three screw-in legs. It was undoubtedly the Reliant Robin of all keyboards.

Rothman's King Size were now a definite thing of the past whilst I saved every penny from my pocket-money and odd jobs that I did for my parents. I vividly remember the

Saturday of purchase. I was actually ten shillings (50p) short of the required amount and so struck a deal with my father to paint his greenhouse at an hourly rate of half a crown (12½p) in order to earn enough to make up the shortfall. After four hours' work I collected my ten shillings and with the rest of my savings set off for Woolworth's at Sudbury Hill to buy the organ. It is also interesting to note that this was the last occasion my father ever asked me to do anything on an hourly rate; in the four hours I worked on his greenhouse I was only able to complete the painting of half of it, which on inspection did not please him particularly.

Once back from my round trip I screwed in the legs of my newly-acquired instrument and broke the thread on the second leg. I jammed matchsticks in to try and secure the leg, which splayed out at a ridiculous angle but nevertheless kept the organ upright.

I plugged it in and switched on. The noise from the fan inside was loud. Louder in fact than the noise the actual notes made. There was also a delay after depressing a note before any sound came. The keys were so small each finger tended to play at least two notes each.

Nevertheless, in my eyes I was now ready to join a band, and I knew the very band that I felt needed my services – the Atlantic Blues.

The Atlantic Blues were a band that had been formed in the Civil Defence hall opposite my parents' house by a lad three years older than me called Ken Holden. Ken was the drummer and his drum kit was made up entirely of borrowed Boys' Brigade drums.

The bass player, Derek, was another local lad and the singer, Paul Sutton, was, along with Ken and me, another member of the 1st Harrow Boys' Brigade. The band also had a part-time guitarist called Alan Leander, whose claim to fame was that his sister knew one of the Who. This was always a very good selling point and never ceased to impress.

"What band you in?"

"The Atlantic Blues."

"Who's in it?"

"Alan Leander is our lead guitarist. His sister knows one of the Who."

"Wow, you must be brilliant."

(No more words were ever necessary after the last statement. I just flashed a knowing smile and moved on.)

Tuesday night was when the Boys' Brigade met, and Ken used to pick us all up in his father's Morris Isis and take us down to South Harrow Church for the meetings. It was on the way home that I delivered my "I want to be in the band" piece.

It was quite simple really. I just waited until an ideal break in the conversation.

"Drill went quite well tonight," said Ken, whilst attempting to turn a corner on two wheels.

"Yes it did," said Paul, "and it'll be a good turn-out at Church Parade next Sunday, too, if everybody there tonight shows up."

"I've got an organ."

Driving off the pavement back on to the road, Ken pulled up at the kerb.

"A real one?"

"Electric."

"Do you want to join the band?"

"I'm not sure, really. I've never thought much about joining a band. Oh, all right, you've talked me into it, I'll give it a go."

I was there early for my first rehearsal. About an hour early as it happens. Ken arrived with his Boys' Brigade drums and Derek with his bass. They seemed suitably impressed with my organ although they had yet to hear it.

Then Alan arrived.

"What's that?"

"My organ."

"That's one of those dreadful Woolworth's jobs. You can't hear them at all. Go on, plug it in and switch it on."

I did as requested, and the noise of the fan seemed to amplify itself around the large Civil Defence hall.

"Now play it," said Alan.

By any standards it was disappointing. There was absolutely nothing you could play on it that would make it sound even remotely acceptable.

"I refuse to stand on the same stage as that organ," announced Alan firmly.

My heart sank. In retrospect, it was a pointless statement anyway, as the band had never performed anywhere in public in its entire existence and prospects in that region were not good as the band was fraught with relatively serious internal musical problems. Ken had a difficulty that affected his drumming quite badly: he couldn't keep time. Derek was unclear on the actual tuning of the bass and Paul was not exactly Mick Jagger when it came to vocals.

We all sat down and took stock of the situation. It was in essence my very first band meeting.

First we took stock of what equipment we had.

Amplification: one Vortexion hundred watt amp with three inputs. One input was loud and the other two were quite simply inaudible. Alan used to plug into the loud socket, Derek into one of the inaudible sockets and one microphone went in the other inaudible socket.

It was very much a guitar-orientated band.

We discussed what we needed.

Drums, for starters. The Boys' Brigade drums had been a useful stop-gap, but in order to be taken seriously we needed the real thing now.

I spoke up.

"I noticed in Woolworth's when I was buying my organ that they had a drum kit for sale. It's called the Gigster Kit and it's forty-nine pounds."

Ken was working as an apprentice at London Transport, and as he was living at home had managed to put a few bob to one side.

"I'll have a look tomorrow," he said.

"If we start getting gear and then get some work we are going to need a van," said Alan.

My word! The knowledge and experience of a man whose sister knew one of the Who was priceless.

"I'll start looking," said Ken.

The subject of my new acquisition was next on the agenda.

"I suppose we could put the microphone over the air holes on the organ when either Paul or myself are not singing," continued Alan, "which would be better than nothing, and also quite a few of the halls where bands play have got pianos, which I suppose would be even better than the organ if we stuff a mike inside."

Then Paul Sutton spoke.

"I don't want to be the singer any more."

Typical, I thought. I've only been in the band half an hour and it's breaking up.

"I think," said Paul, "that Alan and Richard should do all the singing."

"And what about you?" asked Ken.

"I want to be the manager."

We were all very impressed. The top bands all had high-powered managers in big offices, so why not us?

We enquired of our newly installed high-powered manager of his plans for the supergroup whose future was now firmly in his grasp. With all eyes eagerly on him, he thought hard for a moment and then replied:

"Well, a lot depends on how much homework I have next week."

The following two weeks were a hive of activity.

First, Ken bought the Gigster drum kit from Woolworth's. It certainly looked impressive, especially when Ken hit the bass drum and the rim shape changed from round to oval and then back to round again. Obviously the sign of a well-made instrument.

Ken then completely demolished his savings by purchasing

a split-windscreen, 1957 Bedford van from U.C.Slim Motors
of Sudbury Town for an all-in price of thirty-five pounds,
including tax and insurance. We painted "The Atlantic
Blues" in big letters down the side of the van which to
our delight became extremely psychedelic after the first
rainfall.

The first rehearsal that took place after all our new
acquisitions was tremendous. Ken still speeded up, but at
least he was now able to rival Alan in volume. Derek and I
were inaudible but looked good. The vocals were still more
shouted than sung in order to get over the poor amplification,
but all in all it was an outstanding leap forward.

Rehearsal over, we inquired of our manager as regards
bookings.

He informed us that he was working on one or two
promising avenues, but that he had not really been able
to follow them up due to having been given extra French
homework.

After a further half-dozen rehearsals, Paul gave us the
news we had all been waiting to hear.

"We are going to support a visiting French band at a pub
near Hayes. There's no payment, but if the manager likes
the band there is a good chance that he'll re-book us with
a fee and possibly a residency."

We rehearsed and rehearsed, until every mistake was still
there but played with supreme confidence.

Eventually the great day arrived, and we pulled up outside
the hall which adjoined the pub. On entering through the side
doors we noticed that the stage was already full up with the
French band's gear.

"You lot set up on the floor," a voice said.

It was the pub manager.

He looked at me very closely.

"How old are you?"

It was at that moment that I had the sudden realisation
that I was about four years too young to even be on licensed
premises.

Lowering my voice to around basso profundo level, I answered him with as much confidence as I could muster.

"Twenty-six."

"What!"

I'd obviously overdone it.

"Er, on the twenty-sixth I'll be nineteen."

He shook his head and walked away.

We now turned to the next crisis in hand, which was that my reed organ had failed miserably, in its first trip in the Bedford van, to arrive in one piece. It had in fact arrived in several pieces.

"How bad is it?" I asked Ken.

"Well, I think this is one of the legs."

It was clear that we had a terminal case on our hands and I had nothing to perform with on my great band début.

I spotted a piano at the end of the hall, and running after the pub manager, enquired whether or not we could use it.

"You can, but you can't move it."

"But it's down the other end of the hall from where the band are going to set up."

"Well, you'll just have to play on your own down the other end then, won't you."

I walked back to where the rest of the band were setting up and filled them in as to what the manager had said. It was unanimously agreed that the final decision as to whether or not I played the piano lay with me.

I weighed up the pros and cons. First the cons: I would have about two hundred people between me and the rest of the band. Secondly, the band would not be able to either see me or hear me and thirdly, I would not be able to either see or hear them.

I looked at the pros. There weren't any.

I decided to play.

We were due to play for twenty minutes starting promptly at seven thirty. The hall was pretty full, mostly teenage males and mostly legless.

We had agreed that Ken was to count in our opening

number, "Johnny B. Good", by giving four beats on the snare. Ken did this admirably, and to a seriously bemused and confused audience we started playing at opposite ends of the hall. I suppose in retrospect it was possibly the very first live stereo performance.

Unfortunately the audience did not seem to appreciate the momentous occasion they were witnessing and decided that perhaps a full-scale fight would be more entertaining.

It was one heck of a fight as it happened. Obviously none of the participants had spoken to the pub's manager before this unscheduled event, as within five minutes most of the piano was up the other end of the hall. This was balanced out, though, by most of Ken's Gigster drum kit arriving down at my end.

This could have sounded the death knell for lesser bands, but within one week we had bounced back with the stunning news from Ken that he had secured a residency for us.

He was a little vague about all the details, but it was guaranteed that we would be the only band performing and although there was no money involved we would be given sandwiches and soft drinks.

Thursday arrived and eventually we were all picked up in the van. The Gigster kit had been glued back together wherever possible and confidence was high. Ken was still being vague about the gig, but we had gleaned from him enough to know that the audience was mainly teenage and it was at a club in Neasden, north London.

Eventually we pulled into Neasden High Road and were confronted by a man in the middle of the road who was jumping up and down on an invisible pogo stick.

"Watch out," shouted Derek, "there's a nutter running around in the middle of the road."

"Drive carefully past him," I suggested.

"Run him over," said Alan.

Ken did none of these three suggestions. To our amazement he stopped alongside this apparent suicidal maniac and slid back the window.

"Hello, Eric," he said, "all the band's here."

Eric ran off down the middle of the road and turned into an open entrance about a hundred yards ahead.

Ken skilfully manoeuvred the van between the two head-on collisions that Eric had caused and turned into the same entrance.

Within seconds the van was completely surrounded by about fifty Down's syndrome teenagers.

"Ken! Where are we, Ken?" I almost whispered the question.

"I'm not getting out," was Derek's contribution.

"I had nothing to do with this," was our manager's contribution.

Alan had never before shown the violent streak that suddenly manifested itself, but eventually, after managing to pull him off Ken, we sat in the back and held a band meeting.

The meeting was actually going nowhere fast. It was nothing more than a shouting match. Anyway it was brought to an abrupt end by a rather large woman banging on the windscreen.

Ken slid back his side window.

"Would you like some help in with your instruments?" she asked kindly. "The children are so looking forward to hearing you play."

"We're here, so we might as well play," said Ken. "Come on, I've been here before. The kids are really friendly."

I looked out at the friendly kids who had discovered discus-throwing with the Bedford's hubcaps.

"They've got a piano as well."

That sealed it for me.

Gingerly we set up the equipment. The kids were very inquisitive and asked loads of questions which, to be honest, we had difficulty in understanding due to their speech difficulties. Luckily the lady who banged on van windows "translated" for us, and a bond began to develop.

The piano was at the other end of the hall. (What was it

with me and pianos?) It was an old, very large upright with a giant iron frame and without wheels. Four of us failed to move it more than a couple of feet.

The lady who banged on van windscreens came to our rescue yet again.

"Roy will move that for you."

We turned round as a huge shadow appeared to do a total eclipse of the entire area in which the four of us and the piano stood.

As one we looked up at Roy. Roy was huge. Roy made the average heavyweight wrestler seem minute.

"Where would you like Roy to put the piano?"

We looked at Roy again.

"Wherever he likes," I said, as heads nodded in agreement all around me.

Roy seemed to know what was wanted without any instructions from us and effortlessly picked the piano up and carried it down to where the rest of the equipment had been set up.

"Thank you very much," I said and Roy smiled and walked over to me and hugged me. He was obviously capable of crushing every bone in my body, but this hug was gentle and one of friendship. I looked around. All the kids were smiling, just standing around, smiling.

"They're waiting for you to start playing," said the windscreen lady.

Alan Leander started playing the intro for "High-heeled Sneakers" and then we all joined in. Ken promptly went into a drum solo in a tempo of his own choosing. I immediately discovered that the piano was wildly out of tune and Derek realised that his bass guitar wasn't working at all. I looked around and was stunned to see all the kids dancing. They were loving it. The piece eventually ground to a halt and they all cheered and clapped as if we were the Rolling Stones.

We played there every Thursday for the next six months and very quickly all grew to love and understand the kids and become their friends. It will undoubtedly remain as one of the highlighted periods of my career.

Alan Leander also worked with a dance band trio that played at weddings, functions and occasionally at working men's clubs. After a few weeks he asked me if I had ever thought about joining such an outfit. "That's where the money is," he told me. "Come and meet Bernie Vick down at the Tithe Farm pub in South Harrow and we'll talk about it."

Bernie Vick was a highly respected local drummer who worked in various dance bands. I knew he worked a lot and got paid for it. This was the big league as far as I was concerned and I wanted in.

I cycled down to the Tithe Farm, arriving a few minutes early for my seven thirty meeting, and walked into the saloon bar where I ordered a half of lager.

"And how old are you?"

Certain things in life were beginning to become a little monotonous.

I threw a counter-punch.

"I'm meeting Bernie Vick here at half-past seven."

The barman gave me a puzzled look, but Bernie's name seemed to have done the trick as he served me my drink. I walked away from the bar with my half and found myself face to face with a man who was the spitting image of a history teacher at my school, Drayton Manor County Grammar.

"Unbelievable!" I said.

"What is?" he parried.

"You're the spitting image of a teacher at my school."

"And what's his name?"

"Mr Crowe. But we call him Little Hitler."

We both laughed.

"And what year are you in?"

I moved in closer, and looking around to make sure that the barman couldn't hear me, answered with a sly grin on my face.

"Fourth year."

He chuckled again.

"And what's your name?"

"Richard Wakeman."

I held out my hand in offer of friendship. He took it, shook it warmly and spoke.

"I'm Little Hitler and I'll see you tomorrow morning after assembly."

He turned round and walked out of the pub at almost the same instant that Alan and Bernie walked in.

"Been here long?" asked Alan.

"Too long," I answered.

He looked puzzled and decided it best not to continue this particular line of questioning.

"This is Bernie Vick."

I shook hands with this tall, thin, softly spoken man and liked him the moment the first words he spoke to me left his lips.

"What can I get you to drink, Rick?"

The pub had quite a sizeable function room attached to it and Bernie had arranged for us to use it and for me to play the piano, I suppose as some form of audition.

Luckily I had had access to all my father's music and had learned quite a few of the standards. This seemed to impress Bernie, who asked me if I was free on the upcoming Saturday. Deep in apparent thought, I scoured my mental diary and, after subconsciously confirming with myself that I was in fact free for every Saturday that coming year, said that I was pretty sure that I was available.

"Great," said Bernie. "We'll have a rehearsal at my house during the week and be ready for the gig at the Ealing Social Club on Saturday. The piano's pretty good there. Oh and by the way, it's three pounds each. Is that OK with you?"

I was dumbstruck. Three pounds was a small fortune. Back then, in 1964, three pounds would give you the choice of buying fourteen gallons of petrol, three hundred Rothman's

King Size or, if you preferred, three hundred and thirty-five pints of bitter.

I cycled home without a care in the world and with no back lights. I was also slightly tiddly. I had truly entered the world of the semi-professional musician.

3

A rose by any other name

Within a few weeks I found I had established myself amongst the local musicians who worked regularly. It has to be said that whilst I would rather have been playing rock and roll, I was now earning around six pounds every week and had saved up enough to purchase a Hohner Pianet and a VOX AC30 amplifier.

I had started to realise that the Atlantic Blues were, sadly, not going to progress beyond top billing at the Neasden club and so at the same time that Alan Leander left the band, I decided to go as well. It was inevitable that the group would fold up sooner or later as Ken especially had found other distractions in his life that were taking up a lot of his time, the main distraction being called Daphne, whom he married a few years later!

The last performance at Neasden was very memorable. Our replacements in the residency were a local Salvation Army brass band. We were going to play for the first hour and then the Salvation Army band would take over for the final hour. We opened with "Walking The Dog" followed by a series of twelve-bar blues. The kids danced round the room and cheered and cheered.

After we had finished our set, the Salvation Army band opened theirs with "Onward, Christian Soldiers", followed by a series of hymns. The kids danced round the room and cheered and cheered.

We knew then that we didn't make it musically.

One of the trumpet players in the Salvation Army band was a talented young West Indian and we got talking after the evening had drawn to a close.

"I'd love to play trumpet and sing in a rock band," he said. "Can I join your band?"

"Well, we're just splitting up," I said.

He looked crestfallen.

"I am thinking of putting my own band together, though."

Telephone numbers were exchanged and we went our separate ways.

Gigs continued on a regular basis with Bernie Vick's band. We now called ourselves the Conchord Quartet, and were very much in demand for local functions. One day, whilst round at Bernie's house, I was introduced to a clarinettist called Terry Beresford who by day worked at Boosey and Hawkes. Terry freelanced in many of the local dance bands but was round at Bernie's with a proposition.

He had been offered a residency at a new working men's club that was being built in Alperton. They wanted a four-piece band and Terry had the job of supplying the unit.

Sensibly, he felt that if he found a working band to start with and then added himself to it, life would be much simpler. The only problem was that Bernie's band was a quartet: myself, Bernie on drums and two guitarists, Alan Leander and Jim Bennett.

The problem was solved instantly by Bernie. Alan was late for the meeting, and by the time he turned up he was no longer in the band. I resolved from that moment on never to be the last to turn up to any band meetings.

The residency at the Alperton Social Club was great fun. It was there I completed my apprenticeship in drinking, and I worked there every weekend for nearly two years.

After a few months Jim and Bernie had a disagreement with Terry and left. They were replaced with a young drummer called Graham Turner, whose major claim to fame was having a grandmother with two thumbs on her right hand, and my cousin Alan, who joined on saxophone.

I was now seventeen and had purchased my first car, a 1957 100E Ford Anglia. In spite of the fact it had no floor, it served me admirably. There was no testing of vehicles in 1966 and it would not be an exaggeration to say that eighty per cent of the cars on the road back then would have failed the MOT test. My Anglia fell comfortably into this category. With four 4x2 planks serving as foot rests in the front it had nearly as much woodworm and dry rot as rust.

I loved driving, though, and on passing my test headed for the A40 at Northolt, which was the local lads' speed-test stretch of road. Preparation took place in the car-park of the Target pub. Pre-preparation took place inside the Target pub.

Finally, the big moment came when we were to find out the true performance rating of my Anglia. Extremely apprehensively I pulled out of the car-park with Ken Holden sitting next to me and two other friends, Pete and Colin Spiers, in the back. Due to the lack of floor Pete and Colin actually sat with their feet sticking out of the two front-door windows.

I remember being very nervous as I had never gone over thirty miles an hour before.

I crunched my way through to top gear (third), and pressed down hard on the accelerator. Due to the wheels being severely unbalanced, violent wheel wobble had appeared at around the twenty-five mile an hour mark. The sweat was now pouring down my neck.

The point at which the speed test came to an end was near the entrance to Northolt RAF base. This gave a stopping distance of about half a mile to the next set of traffic-lights.

As we approached the airport the exhaust system collapsed and the noise became deafening. Exhaust fumes poured in through the floor as the vibration from the wheels became uncontrollable. Pete and Colin went very quiet.

"Keep going!" screamed Ken. "You're nearly there!"

"How fast are we going?" I screamed back.

"Thirty-three!"

We passed the airport entrance and I slammed my foot on the brake pedal. The back wheels locked and we gracefully slid sideways down towards the traffic-lights where we came to a stop facing the oncoming traffic.

"Terrific!" said Ken.

"I think the brakes may need a slight adjustment," said Colin.

"Shall we go back and pick up the exhaust?" asked Pete.

"Drive your car into the lay-by over there and show me your driving licence and insurance," said the policeman.

After inspecting the vehicle thoroughly, the nice policeman suggested that we could probably salvage the number plates, but the metal, filler and rust between them was almost certainly beyond help.

To be fair, he was right. The Anglia survived for only a few more months and during that period became very temperamental and unreliable. My father had a beautiful Standard Ensign and kindly loaned me the car to go to gigs whenever the Anglia misbehaved. It was during one of these "loan" occasions that the case of "The school concert and the headmaster's rose garden" (still a legendary story amongst the surviving staff at Drayton Manor) took place.

The fact that I now played in a band was pretty well known at school, although it has to be said that I hadn't actually made it clear what type of band it was. The general impression was that the Conchord Quartet was a rock band, and who was I to dispel such thoughts?

Then I was approached by the head of the school dance committee, John Ralph, and the deputy headmaster, Mr Wright.

"Wakeman," said Mr Wright, "as you know, the school dance is fast approaching and I thought it would be a good idea if this year we not only played records but also had a live band. John here tells me you have a very successful group and so we thought it a good idea to see if you were available. There is a payment, of course, as I realise that perhaps some of the group may be professional. The school dance fund has thirty-five pounds for this purpose."

I nearly collapsed. Thirty-five pounds was an absolute fortune. I mentally weighed up the pros and cons as quickly as I could. First the cons: the Conchords were totally unsuitable as I could not see the sixth-formers getting off on the Hokey Cokey and "Knees up, Mother Brown". That meant I had no band. Now the pros: there was a firm gig and thirty-five pounds.

"I'm sure I can talk the lads into doing it," I said confidently. "We don't usually do school dances, but I'm sure I can talk the band into doing it just this once."

"That's settled then," said Mr Wright, and walked off.

Word spread like wildfire around the school. Every spare second of the day seemed to be taken up with my answering questions about the group, and before I knew what was happening the "John's got a black dog" syndrome took over.

The "John's got a black dog" syndrome is a nightmare once it gets going. It's based on the situation of Fred telling Bill that John's got a black dog. Bill then tells Terry that John's been bitten by a huge black dog. Terry tells Harry that John was bitten by a giant black dog which ate him, and so on and so on.

By the end of the week, my band was second only in stature to the Rolling Stones and was about to sign a recording deal with a major American recording company. My band was also fronted by a famous black American soul singer from New York who was flying in specially for the gig.

With two weeks to go to the school dance, all I had was myself, my Hohner Pianet, my VOX AC30 amplifier and an awful lot of worry.

I decided on the Terry Beresford principle as regards getting a band together. I contacted a great friend, Trevor

Alvy, who played rhythm guitar for a local rock band in Harrow, and booked them for fifteen pounds, including a rehearsal day for me to learn their set. I explained to them that for this particular gig they would have to work-under a different name, "Curdled Milk". (This name was all I could come up with when asked by the deputy head what the name of the band was and if we played any Cream numbers.)

Things were going well. I had a band organised and I was still twenty pounds ahead of the game. All I needed now was a black American soul singer from New York.

I looked through my phone book and came up with the next best thing.

A West Indian Salvation Army trumpet player from Neasden.

I called him and explained the situation. He was well up for it, especially for three pounds. The only problem was that he couldn't make the rehearsal, but he did know "Johnny B. Good" and "My Babe", both of which were in the set.

I said this would be no problem as I would find some way of him doing just the two numbers.

The rehearsal went very well. The band that I had "joined" were really pretty good and knew all the necessary twelve bars that all the bands usually played, and they also started and finished pretty much together. A couple of them also had quite long hair, which was a bonus.

The day of the school dance arrived. Tickets had gone like hot cakes and for the first time in the school's history tickets had been sold to other schools in the area. It was going to be jam-packed. By now, my band had signed the big record contract and were about to negotiate a massive tour of the USA with the Who as our possible support band.

For a band that had never played a note in public, Curdled Milk was now the biggest name in west London, and I was about to make seventeen pounds clear profit.

Who needs A-levels?

The Anglia decided not to start and so, thanks to my father's generosity, I loaded my Pianet and amplifier into his Standard Ensign and set off for the school, picking up Trevor Alvy and a couple of the other guys on the way. We had a bit of time to spare and so we decided to stop off at the White Hart in Hanwell for a swift pint.

The swift pint turned into a mini drinking session and we were all a little light-headed by the time we pulled into the school gates. I attempted a hand-brake turn across the playground and found myself skidding totally out of control towards the headmaster's prize rose garden, on which the Standard Ensign finally came to rest.

It was pretty dark and time was against us somewhat, so we unloaded the equipment we had in the car and took it into the main hall and set up. The deputy headmaster was already there and seemed very impressed.

"As this is out of school time, Wakeman," he said, "I think it would be fine for you to park your car in the headmaster's space."

"He already has," said Trevor.

I glared at him.

"Oh, fine. Well, that's OK then."

He walked away.

"They'll never know," said Trevor. "We'll be packed up and gone long before they discover what's happened to the headmaster's rose garden."

I was not convinced, but my thoughts now turned to the dance which was due to start at any minute. Mr Wright had explained to me that he wanted to make a short announcement to open the proceedings. He walked up to the microphone.

"Hello, boys and girls."

His welcome was met with silence.

"All I want to say is that I just want you all to enjoy yourselves tonight and behave like proper young ladies and gentlemen. Snogging will not be allowed and nobody is to leave the hall until the dance is over at ten o'clock. Now it's over to the group – Curdled Milk."

We burst into "Whole Lotta Shakin'" and it was immediately clear that the evening was going to work well. We finished the first piece and I walked up to the microphone.

"Hi there."

I got a cheer.

"As many of you are aware, tonight we have a very special soul singer from America joining us. He is here in the building but, as I'm sure you all understand, he is very tired after such a long journey." (There was an element of truth in this as his bus was late leaving Neasden High Road.) "At present he is recuperating backstage so that he can do the last part of the evening with us."

This announcement was met with approving and understanding nods, and the dance continued with only one interruption which came at about nine o'clock.

We had just finished "Not Fade Away" and were about to launch ourselves into "Peggy Sue" when Mr Wright appeared on the stage.

He walked over to me.

"I'm sorry about this, Wakeman, but I have to make an important announcement."

He walked up to the microphone.

"I am very sorry to have to interrupt such a great evening, but as usual there is always somebody who wants to spoil everything for everybody else and until I have resolved the matter satisfactorily the dance will not continue."

Groans.

He continued.

"Some stupid, inconsiderate maniac has driven his car on to the headmaster's prize rose garden, completely destroying it."

Howls of laughter.

"This is no laughing matter. The perpetrator has even had the cheek to leave his car on the garden."

More howls.

"Unless the perpetrator of this disgraceful act makes

himself known to me immediately, I shall have no alternative but to end the dance here and now."

I slowly got up from behind the Hohner Pianet and walked up to Mr Wright.

"Er. Excuse me, sir."

"Not now, Wakeman. I know this must be very disappointing for you, but I have to get to the bottom of this."

He returned to the microphone.

"This is your last chance, whoever you are. The vehicle registration number is BFJ 974."

I stepped forward again.

"Sit down, Wakeman!" he bellowed.

"It's my car!" I bellowed back.

He looked at me in stunned amazement.

"It was an accident, sir. Honest it was."

He turned and faced me.

"Well, it's unfair that the school dance should suffer because of your stupidity, so I'll deal with you tomorrow after assembly."

It rather took the shine off my evening, but we soon got back into the swing of things.

At half-past nine I played my trump card.

"Ladies and gentlemen. Would you please welcome the greatest singer ever to come out of New York, Soul Man Wesley!

The place went wild.

So did Wesley, for that matter. He was quite brilliant. He strutted up and down the stage and sang his two party pieces whilst rolling around the floor and going totally over the top. The evening was a roaring success.

Reality hit home, though, as I reversed off the headmaster's rose garden. Quite a lot of the roses were now an integral part of the front grille of the Standard Ensign, and even in the dark I could see that things were pretty terminal in the floral department.

After assembly the following morning, I was summoned into the headmaster's office.

To this day I have never fully understood how one man could be so passionate over roses. He was actually crying as he forced me to witness the carnage that I had unfortunately been responsible for.

Repeated mutterings of apology plus pleas that it really was an accident failed in any respect to be accepted as mitigation.

"You will pay for the damage, Wakeman."

"Yes, sir."

"I have had it assessed by the gardener and it will cost you twenty-five pounds."

"I don't have twenty-five pounds, sir."

"In that case I shall write to your parents."

"How long have I got to find it, sir?"

"You haven't. I want it immediately."

Mr Wright interjected.

"I have here the envelope with the thirty-five pounds owed to Wakeman for his group who played at the school dance last night, sir. May I suggest that we take twenty-five pounds from that and give Wakeman the balance?"

"Good idea. Is that agreeable to you, Wakeman?"

"Well, actually, sir, that won't leave me enough to pay the band."

They just looked at me.

"But it does seem the best thing to do in the circumstances, I suppose."

"That's settled, then."

I left the headmaster's office with a new problem – how to pay a band fifteen pounds and a soul singer from Neasden three pounds when you only had ten pounds. The problem was eventually solved by paying three pounds to Wesley and seven to the band. I then paid them the eight pound balance over the following two weeks from my earnings with the Conchord Quartet.

Curdled Milk never ever performed again.

4

Another Rank certainty

Life carried on at the Borough of Brent Social Club in Alperton, and after a year Terry left and I took over the band. Instead of replacing Terry and bringing in another musician, we decided to continue as a trio, thereby giving ourselves a pay rise.

Graham, the drummer, was a service engineer for Hammond organs and when he asked me if I'd like to go with him to the Top Rank ballroom at Watford, to service their big C3 Hammond, I jumped at the chance. I had only ever seen pictures of the C3 in magazines and was very keen to see one up close. Graham had hinted that if there was no one around I could possibly even have a go on it.

It transpired that it actually belonged to the bandleader, Ronnie Smith. Graham had never met him, but told me that the band was very highly rated. It was a twelve-piece and made up mainly of session men.

I can vividly remember walking into the ballroom. It was huge. It must have held at least two thousand people.

"It's full every Thursday, Saturday and Sunday," Graham told me.

A guy in a black suit and bow tie took Graham and me over to the stage area.

"Where's the organ?" I asked Graham.

"They'll turn the stage round in a minute," he said.

I stood wide-eyed whilst the stage revolved, revealing an area covered in music stands, microphones, amplifiers and, of course, the Hammond C3.

Graham switched it on. It purred into life. Graham unscrewed the back to reveal trays of wires and immediately started fiddling amongst them.

"Is something wrong with it?" I enquired.

"No, nothing," said Graham, "but Ronnie Smith will ask the guy who brought us over to the stage what I did, and if he sees the back off the organ he'll assume something's being done to it."

After about ten minutes, Graham replaced the back and motioned to me.

"Go on, have a go."

"I'd better not."

"There's no one around, go on, have a go."

I slid on to the bench and started playing "Green Onions." It was fabulous. Loud and fabulous. I got carried away, pulled a few more drawbars out and started into a blues.

"Oi! You two! What do you think you're playing at?"

I looked up and saw a man in his early thirties standing on the dance floor just below the stage.

I froze, but Graham managed to keep some sort of composure and calmly said, "I'm from Hammond's. I've just repaired the C3 and my friend here is testing it for me."

"Well, I'm Ronnie Smith. This is my Hammond and I don't like people playing it."

He clambered up on to the stage and stood behind the organ, looking straight at me.

"Can you read music?"

"Er, yes."

"In the organ stool you're sitting on you'll find a large folder with lots of numbered music in it. Take it out."

I did as he asked and waited for my next instructions.

"Right. Find number thirty-two and play it for me."

I found number thirty-two and played it for him.

"Now number sixty-six."

I found sixty-six and played that for him.

This puzzling scenario continued in a similar manner for about fifteen minutes. Finally Ronnie asked me if I worked for Hammond's.

I explained that I was actually at school doing my A-levels before, I hoped, going on to college, and that Graham and I played in a band together.

"Would you like to work here?" Ronnie said to me.

My mouth opened but no sound came out.

"Thursday, Saturday and Sunday. Twelve pounds. Start next Thursday."

"But I have a residency at weekends," I blurted out.

"Where at?"

I paused before answering, looking around at the magnificent ballroom I was in and at the Hammond I was sitting at. I also thought of twelve pounds every week.

"It's a club in Alperton. I've been there nearly two years now."

"Time to move on, then. Give them two weeks' notice."

On the Thursday of my first performance at the Top Rank, my mother had insisted that I look smart. I had been forced into a haircut that was terrifyingly short and into my one and only, ill-fitting, suit.

I arrived one hour early at the Top Rank ballroom and made my way to the band room. Getting no reply after knocking, I opened the door and went in. There was a hanging rail going the complete length of one wall with a selection of bright blue and orange jackets hanging from it. There were a dozen or so chairs against the remaining walls and a door leading to a toilet.

I looked at my watch. There were only ten minutes before the band was due on stage. I could hear the dee-jay playing records and I knew there were a lot of people in, but I was the only band member who appeared to be in the building.

Just as I was about to panic the door burst open and eleven

guys poured in. Some were laughing and joking and some just went straight to the hanging rail and picked off a jacket. All had drinks in their hands and most had long hair. They also all had clothes that fitted them.

The last man through the door had the longest hair I had ever seen. He was dressed in really wild clothes and had a large Scotch in one hand and a pint in the other. He was chattering away to another guy who was also wildly dressed, and then he saw me.

He stared at me for about a minute and then said, "Is this another of Henry's jokes?"

I later learned that Henry was the band's nickname for Ronnie Smith.

Ronnie Smith appeared in the doorway.

"What's the matter with you, Ashley?"

The guy called Ashley spoke again.

"Who's this, Henry? Another one of your cheap musicians just so you can keep the required number on stage to please Top Rank?"

"Ashley, this is our new organist."

Groans all round.

"Look at him, Henry. You must be joking. Where were you playing before this?" he asked me.

"The Borough of Brent Social Club."

He turned back to Ronnie Smith.

"Wonderful. Henry! You've gone too far this time."

Ashley walked up to me.

"Who cut your hair? The council?"

Another voice piped up. "Leave him alone. He'll be out on his ear next week."

"Henry, his clothes don't even fit him."

Ronnie Smith put his hands up.

"Look, you lot. He's in the band. His name is Rick and you're on in three minutes. Rick, take a jacket off the rail. It'll be the one with no name on the inside. Write your name on it somewhere and then you'll know it's yours, and get down on the bandstand with everybody else ready for the stage to revolve. We'll start with number thirty-five. *Now move it*!"

At that moment I couldn't remember ever feeling so miserable in my entire life. I went over to the rail and took the blue band jacket with no name on it. It was, in fact, the only jacket left. Obviously the way the system worked was that when somebody left, their name was removed from the inside and the new recruit took the jacket.

I was six foot four, weighed approximately twelve stone, had long arms and a thirty-two-inch waist.

Although I never met the guy who left the band just before I joined, I can confidently confirm that he was five foot three, weighed about seventeen stone, had no arms and a forty-six-inch waist.

I hung the jacket on my shoulders and walked down the stairs on to the bandstand. The band looked at me in stunned amazement.

"Henry, he's actually found a jacket that makes his own clothes look good."

I was now close to tears. I was seventeen, very raw around the gills, and about to play in front of two thousand people with a band made up almost entirely of London's top session men. The biggest gig I had ever done up to this point was the London Irish New Year's Eve party in London with the Conchord Quartet, where we played to five hundred legless Irishmen who had no idea what day it was.

The dee-jay poked his head round the curtain.

"Ronnie, this is the last record, I'm handing over to you in about twenty seconds. Oh, and by the way, the Bushey mob are in and looking for a fight."

"Thanks," said Ronnie and as the record came to an end, counted us in to "Soul Finger."

Ronnie pressed a button by the side of the stage and the stage started revolving.

I was pumped up beyond belief. My part was dead easy for "Soul Finger" and so I could relax a bit. I was playing just what was written as I didn't want to upset anybody by embroidering my part.

The stage stopped revolving. I looked out at about a thousand people on the dance floor and another thousand on the balconies.

The lights were not very bright and I was initially intrigued by the "way out" style of dancing that seemed to be happening on the dance floor directly in front of me, but shortly after the first bottle smashed against the side of the organ I realised that they were in fact fighting and not trying out the latest dance craze.

Within ten seconds it was a riot. Bouncers appeared from everywhere, but seemed to be more intent on keeping the fight going than stopping it.

Ronnie pressed the button and the stage revolved back round as "Soul Finger" ground to a halt. The dee-jay appeared and put Brahms' lullaby on the turntable to try and sooth things a little. It had totally the opposite effect. So much so that I can fully recommend it to the Boxing Board of Control to play before the next British heavyweight contender takes the ring for a world title fight. I guarantee it will incite him, perhaps even as far as round two!

I slid off the organ stool. The band seemed entirely unmoved by what was going on and, laughing and joking with each other, climbed the stairs to the band room.

I was flabbergasted.

Ronnie turned to me to explain.

"That doesn't happen very often. Just when the Bushey mob come looking for the Watford mob. It'll be all over in about fifteen minutes and we'll get back on. We've got three sets to do; the first will just be a little short, that's all."

I was last into the band room, where all the guys stood surrounding a tall, extremely scantily dressed girl holding a tray. Between her cries of "Stop that, Ashley" and "I'm not coming in here again", I gathered she was taking the band's order for drinks.

"What do you want, Rick?"

A guy I recognised as the bass player was looking at me. His name was Ken Rankin, and I discovered later that the girl taking the orders was his girlfriend.

"Well, what are you drinking?"

"That's very kind of you. A pint of bitter, please."

One of the guitarists, Rod Freeman, walked over to me.

"Listen, Rick. Ken's not buying, just ordering. We all pay for our own drinks."

"I'll still have a pint of bitter, please," I said.

"That'll be five shillings [25p]," said Norma.

I stared in disbelief. At the Borough of Brent Social Club it was a third of that price. I only had ten shillings with me, but I couldn't back down now.

"Fine," I said, and gave her my ten-shilling note.

"If you're having the same after the next set, I might as well hang on to the change and then we're all square," she said.

I gave a nonchalant smile of acceptance, trying to appear as cool as possible, and sat down on one of the chairs.

One of the sax players, Lenny, came and sat next to me.

"Don't worry too much about all the verbal they're slinging at you, they do it all the time. Especially Ashley. He's a great rock singer and Henry doesn't want to lose him, which is why Ash can answer him back so much."

A voice piped up from my other side. It was the drummer.

"I'm Terry, the deputy bandleader, which means that I take all the flack from Henry for an extra ten shillings a week."

He then went on to explain, in very colourful language, why Ronnie should be put to death by slow torture as his penance for treating the band so badly.

The drinks arrived at the same time as Ronnie ordered us back on to the bandstand. Drinks were not allowed on stage.

The fight had finished, and the stage revolved to reveal a sea of dancers and a dozen or so girls trying to touch Ashley as he strutted up and down the stage.

I was now really enjoying myself. The parts were actually quite easy.

"Forty-two," shouted Ronnie.

I found forty-two. It was "Blueberry Hill".

I quickly scoured the part before Ronnie counted it in and saw a sixteen-bar section marked "organ solo". My heart skipped a beat. Here was a chance to show off a bit, maybe impress and perhaps even make friends and secure my position within the band.

Just before Ronnie started counting he shouted to Rod Freeman, "Take the organ solo, Rod."

I couldn't believe it. Nevertheless I tried to put on a brave face, although deep down I was feeling bitterly disappointed.

My favourite definition of all time is one that I heard on a Christian radio station in mid-America during the Yes Union tour, and it concerns luck.

"Luck," the unidentified voice said through the car radio speaker, "is when preparation meets opportunity." I was knocked out with this definition, and I can remember pulling my van over to the side of the road and mentally applauding before writing down what I had just heard.

What was about to happen to me in the Top Rank ballroom at Watford was to become a perfect example of that definition.

Midway through the first verse, I realised that something had changed in the band's sound. The lead guitar had stopped playing. I looked over at Rod and saw that he had broken his top E-string.

Rod unstrapped his guitar and starting unwinding the machine head holding the broken string. I looked back at my part and realised that the solo sections were a mere twelve bars away and that Rod was not going to have a new string on and tuned in that time. I naturally presumed that the rhythm guitarist would take the solos, so settled down to the block chords that were written in front of me.

Out of the corner of my eye I saw Ronnie attract Ashley's

attention and point at me. Ash came over to the organ and said, "Take the first solo."

Before I had time to even acknowledge him the first solo section had arrived and I went for it with everything I'd got. Fast runs, blues licks and smears, you name it and I fitted it into the sixteen bars.

During the final bar I relaxed and looked up to where Ashley had been standing. He was no longer there. He was in fact standing on top of Ronnie's organ.

"Take the guitar solo as well!" screamed Ashley.

"Get off my organ!" screamed Ronnie.

It was a totally different band in the dressing-room after that set. They all talked to me for starters! Ashley and Rod pulled me to one side.

"What do you think?" said Ashley, looking me up and down.

"He's a visual disaster," said Rod.

"We can work on that," said Ashley. "Do you know Hendrix, Rick?"

I said that I knew most of Hendrix's stuff but as there was no organ in the Jimi Hendrix Experience I hadn't learned any of the music.

"We could adapt some stuff for the weekend. It'd be really good, you know, Henry."

"Fine by me," said Ronnie.

"I'll give you my address after the last set and we'll meet up tomorrow morning at my place. OK with you, Rod?"

Rod nodded approvingly.

I felt great, except I had that nagging feeling in my stomach that told me I should be somewhere else tomorrow morning. Ah yes, I remembered. I had an A-level art lesson. In my excitement I had forgotten to mention to the band that I was still at school! However, this did not seem the ideal time to broach the subject and so I concentrated on my pint that had been brought in on a tray with everybody else's drinks.

The final set was really enjoyable. Ronnie had told me to take a solo whenever he pointed at me, and it seemed he was pointing at me every couple of minutes. I didn't mind, I was having a ball.

I hung up my band jacket and set off for the car-park in order to drive home. Ashley chased after me.

"Here's my address and telephone number," he said. "Give me a ring in the morning and I'll give you proper directions."

I drove back to my parents' house in seventh heaven. I felt sure I had secured my position in the band and hadn't a care in the world.

How unbelievably naïve I was.

(And still am, for that matter!)

After breakfast on Friday morning I phoned Ashley. My parents had both left for work and I had decided that I could get away with missing art just this once.

I got my directions and drove out to Amersham where I had arranged to meet Ashley at his father-in-law's news-agent's.

I pulled up outside the shop at about ten o'clock. Ashley met me there and, on his instructions, I followed him upstairs to the flat above the shop, where in the lounge an elderly man was slumped fast asleep in an armchair, snoring violently.

"That's the father-in-law," said Ash. "He gets up real early to do the papers and always has a swift two hours' sleep about now before going back down to the shop. Just take a pew on the sofa and I'll be back in about ten minutes. Then we'll scoot off to my place."

I sat down opposite Ashley's father-in-law and waited. He was certainly out for the count.

The door opened and I rose, ready to leave, thinking it was Ashley, but instead a small boy of about three years of age entered the room. He was holding an empty milk bottle.

He toddled over to me and stared.

I didn't want to get the kid talking and wake the father-in-law, but felt I had to acknowledge him somehow, and so I tried smiling at the little lad.

He seemed totally unmoved by this proposal of friendship and toddled over to the sleeping father-in-law.

"Gang-dad," he said, pointing at his sleeping grandpa.

I smiled and, putting my finger to my lips, gave him my best "Keep quiet and don't wake Gang-dad" look.

"Milk bokkle," said the little boy.

I smiled again and nodded.

The little boy then smashed the milk bokkle over Gang-dad's head and toddled out.

I sat in total amazement as blood poured out of a gaping cut in the now unconscious Gang-dad's forehead.

As if on cue, Ashley walked in.

Unable to speak I pointed at Gang-dad, who I was reasonably convinced was dead.

Ashley stuck his head back round the door and shouted down the stairs.

"Duchess!" (This was Ashley's pet name for his wife.) "Julian's crowned your father with a milk bottle again, can you sort it out?"

He beckoned to me.

"Come on. This happens all the time. The Duchess will sort it out."

Passing a very relaxed-looking Duchess on the stairs, we walked passed little Julian still clutching a broken milk bottle.

Ashley carefully took it from him and said, "Naughty Julian. You mustn't do that. Grandad doesn't like being hit on the head."

"Gang-dad bleeding," said little Julian.

We drove to Ashley's mum's house a couple of miles away, where we met Rod. Ashley had brought some Hendrix records with him and we put them on the record-player.

"We'll have to re-arrange the tracks if we're going to try and do cover versions," I said.

"No problem," said Ashley.

"Ronnie will never let us do Hendrix stuff. He says the kids won't dance to it and there's nothing for the brass section to play."

"Henry will go for it if I tell him that the manager at the Top Rank is a Hendrix freak," said Ashley. "Henry loves scoring brownie points."

"The manager at the Top Rank is in his forties and thinks Hendrix is a make of washing machine," countered Rod.

"Look," said Ashley, "I'm fed up with all the soul and pop stuff all the time. We need to do something different. I can talk Henry round if we learn the stuff."

And so we did.

We learned "Purple Haze", "All Along the Watchtower" and "Hey, Joe".

We arrived early at the Top Rank the following day and met Terry the drummer and Ken the bass player to rehearse. We had decided not to tell Ronnie we were ready until we had thoroughly rehearsed the new arrangements.

Come the following Thursday we were ready. There was an idea we had for "Hey, Joe" which we felt we should tell Ronnie about, but first we played him "Purple Haze".

He seemed impressed, especially as all the brass section applauded and cheered wildly.

The real reason the brass section applauded and cheered wildly was, of course, that it meant they could sneak off for a quick drink during the Hendrix medley if Ronnie included it in the set.

We played a bit of "All Along the Watchtower" and after a minute Ronnie stopped us.

"Yeah. All sounds good to me," he said.

"There's one more, Ronnie," I said. "'Hey, Joe'".

"I'm sure it's fine," said Ronnie. "All back here at eight o'clock, ready for the first set."

"Ronnie," said Ashley, "there's an idea we've got for 'Hey, Joe' and we'd like to talk to you about it before we go ahead."

"Ashley," said Ronnie, "I'm busy. Do whatever you have to do and don't bother me with trivialities."

We shrugged our shoulders and went off to the bar. We overheard Ronnie chatting to the manager.

"I've got the lads to learn some Hendrix," said Ronnie nonchalantly.

"I think the wife's got one of his washing machines," replied the manager.

Ronnie had decided to save the Hendrix until the third set of the evening, as he reckoned that would be the spot where it would have the most impact. He had also convinced the manager to listen to the Hendrix numbers and watch the audience reaction.

Halfway through the third set, Ronnie whispered to Ashley to start the Hendrix medley whilst he went and got the manager from his office. The brass section left for the bar.

The kids on the dance floor, realising that something a bit different was about to happen, crowded round the front of the stage.

We burst into "Purple Haze". At its conclusion we received quite a decent reception. "All Along the Watchtower" also went down pretty well. Throughout both these pieces, though, we had been unable to spot Ronnie or the manager, so we carried on into "Hey, Joe".

"Hey, Joe" was really my chance to solo myself to death. We had worked out a few nice visual effects which involved doing things to Ronnie's organ, but as he hadn't given us a chance to explain our ideas to him I said to Ashley that we should perhaps leave it out until another time.

"Like heck we will," said Ashley. "Go for it."

I was actually in the middle of going for it when I spotted Ronnie in the top balcony with the manager.

I was able to spot him quite clearly as I was nearly the same height as the balcony. This was due to the fact that Ronnie's organ was now on its side with me standing on it playing "smears" with a giant broom.

I could see Ronnie was not overwhelmed. I couldn't exactly hear what he was saying, but as he kindly repeated

it later in the band room I learned that I was quite correct
in my original surmise to Ashley that it was pretty rude.

In fairness, Ronnie was in a difficult position. The crowd
had loved it. Therefore the manager had loved it. That all
added to Ronnie's security within the Top Rank set-up, and
so, for the time being anyway, Ronnie loved it.

I stayed at the Top Rank, Watford, for nearly a year. Then
one day Ronnie asked me if I would do the dinner-dances as
well as the three rock nights. I explained to Ronnie I was
finishing my A-levels and it really wasn't possible to take any
more time off – I was sitting the exams that month, and I had
to pass in order to get into the Royal College of Music. It also
has to be said that I hated the dance band music. I had done
a couple of the functions for Ronnie and it was all too jazzy
for my taste, so I kept myself amused by getting drunk as
early on in the evening as humanly possible in order to help
the time pass quickly!

Ronnie fully understood my position and gave me one
week's notice.

I was devastated. So for that matter were Ashley and the
rest of the band. They all appealed to Ronnie, but in vain –
he was adamant. He couldn't afford to pay two organists each
week. He needed one who would do both jobs for him.

As I left the Top Rank for the last time, Lenny Case, one
of the saxophone players, chased after me.

"Here, Rick," he said. "Ring this number and ask for Dave
Simms. He's a mate of mine who runs a showband and I hear
they're looking for a new organist."

"Thanks, Lenny," I said, "but I don't have my own
organ."

"I think they supply everything," he countered. "Give it
a go, you've got nothing to lose."

The following morning I took time off from A-level
revision and dialled the number Lenny had given me.

The number rang a couple of times and then a voice at
the other end said, "Musical Bargain Centre, Dave Simms
speaking. Can I help you?"

"I'm a friend of Lenny's, the sax player at the Top Rank, Watford. He told me to give you a ring. My name's Rick Wakeman. I'm the organist Ronnie Smith's just sacked."

"Ah yes. Lenny called me late last night. He said you're a bit good and just what we're looking for. Can you come round and see me? I've got a music shop in South Ealing."

Forty-five minutes later, I was to walk through the door of a second-hand-instrument shop that was to play a very important part in the next stage of my musical apprenticeship.

5

Call my bluff

Dave Simms was the real musician's friend. His shop was mostly made up of second-hand amplifiers, guitars, basses and speaker cabinets. He would always manage to do a deal somewhere along the line for a budding young musician, however lacking in money he might be.

Dave also ran the Tony Dee Showband. To this day I have no idea where the name came from. There was certainly no Tony Dee.

I never really did an audition, just a rehearsal. The band consisted of a two-piece brass section, bass player, guitarist, drummer, myself on organ (a double-manual Vox Continental) and a female singer. The music was very varied and the band was pretty well booked up with high-class functions all around the London area. The money was not as good as what I had been earning at the Top Rank as we only worked a couple of nights a week, but I really enjoyed playing with the band and Dave and I became great friends.

After a few months I found myself at the Royal College of Music and after a few more months found myself spending most of my spare time at the Musical Bargain Centre. Dave had clientele from many of the top bands, John Entwhistle from the Who being a notable example. The shop was always buzzing, and Dave let me play on any gear that came in.

It was early 1968. I was in my second term at the Royal College and was already seriously disillusioned with life there.

This particular morning, I had stopped off at the Bargain Centre for a quick coffee on my way into college for my art of music lecture with Antony Hopkins.

Ernie, Dave's right-hand man, and I were discussing the merits of Hammond organs and why I couldn't afford the second-hand L100 they had in the shop, when the door opened and a young guy with a mop of dark curly hair walked in.

"Hello, Chas," said Dave. "What can I do for you?"

"A set of my usual gauge Rotosound strings, please, for the Fender jazz bass."

Ernie handed a set over to him.

"How's it going, Chas?"

"Right now it's a nightmare." He put the strings in his pocket and gratefully took the mug of coffee that Dave handed him. "I'm working with a black soul singer by the name of Jimmy Thomas at the moment. He's actually the male singer with the Ike and Tina Turner band and Denny Cordell, the producer, has brought him over to England to record some solo stuff. The problem is that half his band have been refused work permits and we're booked in the studio Friday week. The biggest headache is that one of the guys who couldn't get a work permit is the organist, who does all the brass arrangements, and so Jimmy's got that problem area to sort out as well. I've got to take the demo tape of the song that needs the arrangements up to Denny's office before midday and then get off to rehearsals."

"I think I can solve your problem," said Dave.

"Really?" said Chas. "Be great if you could."

"I know an organist who also does great arrangements and who I know could do everything that's needed, and won't cost you an arm and a leg."

I looked at Dave. I was very impressed. This guy must know everybody.

"Where can I find this guy?" asked Chas.

"He's here. Meet Rick."

I took Chas's proffered hand, unable to speak.

"I'll get the tape out of my car. Be back in a jiffy."

I stood rooted to the spot, but managed to aim a sentence at Dave.

"Are you mental? I've only done a few band arrangements and they were for the showband."

"What's the difference? You can do it."

Chas returned with a small spool of quarter-inch tape and a piece of paper with a telephone number written on it.

"Here's my number, Rick. Let me have yours and I'll call you later today and give you details of where the session is going to be and at what time. I'll also let you know where the arrangements have got to be sent. Must go."

And he went.

I missed the art of music lecture. I went home to play the tape on my extremely cheap Hi Fidelity tape-recorder. The track sounded great even in demo form and I had a couple of ideas almost immediately on what to do with the brass parts. Then I realised that I had no idea how many musicians I was writing for or what brass instruments they wanted to use. I called Chas and asked for more details on the line-up.

His reply contributed immensely to what I was convinced was about to be my first coronary.

"Well, I spoke to Jimmy and he's knocked out that you're doing the arrangements and playing the organ as well. I've told him you're very experienced, and so he wants you to book the musicians for him. He wants a six-piece brass section of two trumpets, two trombones and two saxes. He also wants you to conduct the session, which incidentally is at Olympic Studios in Barnes at ten o'clock Friday week. See you there, Rick."

See me there? I didn't even know where the place was. I'd never been in a studio in my life and had no idea how on earth I went about booking musicians.

College went by the wayside for that week. Officially I was

ill. In reality I just felt ill. I was terrified. I had written the
arrangements, which I was quite happy with, and had copied
out all the parts myself, which had taken me ages. I had also
contacted Lenny, from the Top Rank. He had kindly put me
in touch with the right session musicians, who seemed totally
unfazed by a call from an unknown teenager offering them
work. They just took down details of where and when the
session was, and rang off.

The big day came, and I arrived at Olympic Studios three
hours early. There was a guy in Reception called Vic Smith
who introduced himself as the engineer. He then looked at
his watch and asked me why I had got there so early. I
mumbled something about meeting Chas for a drink and
he seemed satisfied with the explanation.

"He'll probably be in the pub over the road, knowing
Chas," said Vic. "I've got to get the studio ready, so if
you'll excuse me I'll see you later."

He vanished up a flight of stairs and I wandered over the
road to the pub, where a couple of large Scotches certainly
helped matters.

I arrived back in the reception area about forty-five
minutes before the session was due to begin and met Chas
coming in the main entrance.

"Hi, Rick. Everything all right? Jimmy's on his way with
the rest of the band. We're going to do the backtrack first
apparently and add the brass around about midnight."

"I've booked the brass players for ten o'clock," I said,
panic starting to set in.

"That's OK. They'll go over the pub until they're wanted.
Let's go up to studio two and see what's set up."

We walked into the control room of studio two and my
jaw nearly hit the ground. I had never even seen a picture of
a studio before and the desk, covered in hundreds of knobs
and faders, just seemed to fill the entire room. There were
flashing lights everywhere, and what space the desk didn't
fill was taken up by the biggest tape machines I'd ever seen.
It was like being in another world.

Vic spoke to me. "Have you used the new Studer before?"
Not having a clue what a Studer was, I plumped for the safest answer.

"No."

I was quite pleased with myself at answering so confidently but was thrown sideways by Vic's next question.

"What have you mainly used, then?"

"Well, all sorts really. You know how it is."

Vic seemed satisfied.

"Yeah, everyone's installing different stuff these days. I think you'll like the Studer, though."

"I'm sure I will," I said, hoping that before the session came to an end I might find out what a Studer was.

We wandered into the recording area, where a drum kit was set up behind some screens and Chas's bass amp stood neatly against a wall already miked up. A magnificent Hammond was on the opposite side to Chas's amp and there was a large conductor's music stand in the middle of the room.

I started to panic.

"You all right?" asked Chas. "You've gone very pale."

"Just a little concerned about the brass parts, to be honest with you, Chas," I said.

"You've done loads of arrangements before, though," said Chas. "Why should this one be any different? It's just another session for you, surely?"

I smiled and asked him where the toilet was.

When I got back, I found Chas, the drummer and the guitarist running through the piece we were to record, which was called "The Running Kind".

In the control room Vic had been joined by three other men, one of them being a black guy who I took to be Jimmy Thomas.

They came into the recording studio and Chas brought them over to me.

"This is Rick," he announced.

I was hit with a barrage of "Hey, man" and "What's

happening, man?" and "Tonight's gonna be really something".

I could relate to the last statement.

They eventually introduced themselves as Denny Cordell,
Tony Visconti and Jimmy Thomas.

"I don't recall seeing you around, Rick. Where have you
been lately?" The question came from Tony, who spoke with
a soft American accent.

The answer, "Finishing my A-levels and attending the
Royal College of Music," didn't seem to fit the bill as to
the reply that was required and so I compromised.

"I've just come back from abroad."

Now this was not a lie. The truth was that I had been
abroad for the first time in my life just a few months earlier.
To be exact, Majorca. I'd been on a forty-nine-pound pack-
age holiday with my mate Peter Wakefield.

"A lot of guys have been in Europe this year," said Tony.
"How did you find it out there?"

"Hot," I said.

They laughed. I failed to understand why, but I seemed to
have bluffed my way successfully through to this stage and
my confidence was beginning to grow.

"Let's get going, then," said Denny. "I've sent the brass
players over to the pub. We should have the track ready for
them in a couple of hours at most."

I sat down at the Hammond and fired her up. I was pretty
excited and the adrenalin was flowing through me at a rate
of knots.

A voice came over the foldback speaker.

"Put your cans on, Rick, and count everybody in."

"Pardon?"

"Put your cans on and count everybody in."

"My cans?"

"Yeah, your cans."

At that moment I began to panic. I was certain I was about
to be caught out as the fraudster I really was. The truth was I
had no idea at all what cans were. There was a Coke can lying

around, but I failed to see how putting that on my head was going to be an aid to the recording.

I went for the "I'm on a different planet" approach.

"Sorry, guys, I must be blind. I can't see the cans anywhere."

"There, right in front of you on top of the organ," the voice from the control room said.

All there was on top of the organ was a set of headphones. I put them on and was relieved to hear a voice in them saying, "Right, count in, in your own time."

"The Running Kind" had a really flash organ opening and in fact had quite a decent part running through it which was not particularly easy to play. The band were tight and it was also the first time I had played with Chas, who really impressed me.

"That's great," Denny's voice came over the foldback. "A couple more run-throughs and we'll start recording. I reckon we'll have it down in three takes at the most, then we'll take a fifteen-minute break whilst we get the brass section back from the pub and miked up."

And that's exactly what happened.

The rhythm section left the studio, their part in the proceedings over with, and I was left alone with Denny, Tony and Jimmy. The brass players arrived from the pub and sat down at their allotted positions.

I handed out the music. They just glanced at their parts, put them on the music stands in front of them and carried on talking to each other. I was very impressed, and starting to feel nervous again.

"Right, let's go for it," said Denny, and he, Tony and Jimmy went back into the control room.

They were in after sixteen bars. I stood behind the conductor's stand, counting through the sixteen bars, waiting to bring the brass section in at the correct place.

I needn't have bothered, though. These guys were real pros. They knew just where their entrance was, and at bar fifteen they all had their lips on their mouthpieces in anticipation. At bar seventeen they all played. It sounded horrendous and ground immediately to a halt.

I was dumbstruck.

"What on earth's going on in there?" came Denny's voice from the control room. "Play it right, guys."

I had a nasty feeling they *were* playing it right. I had a very nasty feeling that they were playing exactly what I had written.

"Let's go again," said Denny.

We did.

With the same result.

The lead trumpet player beckoned to me.

I walked over to him.

"Who did the copying, kid?"

"I did it myself," I answered.

"You've forgotten to transpose the parts."

I wanted to die on the spot. There was no escape. In my enthusiasm when writing the arrangements, I had totally forgotten to write the brass parts in their transposed keys. There was no way out of this one. It would take four or five hours at least to recopy the parts. I was about to be found out, big-time.

The lead trumpet player whispered in my ear: "It's OK, kid, we'll save you." He turned to the other five guys. "It's all written in concert pitch, guys. Transpose accordingly."

And they did, and it sounded wonderful.

The trumpet player's name was Kenny Baker, one of Britain's most famous session players. To him I will be eternally grateful.

The session over, I picked up the music and went into the control room to say goodbye and thank you to Vic, Tony, Denny and Jimmy.

Denny beckoned me in.

"You're a fine player and arranger, Rick, and I want to talk to you about some ideas I've got. Come and see me on Monday morning at eleven o'clock in my office."

He handed me his card, which had "Denny Cordell, Regal Zonophone" and an address printed on it.

I put it in my top pocket and walked down the stairs.

The "Music of the Sixteenth Century" lecture was going to be one short on Monday morning.

6

Out on my own

Dumbarton House, 68 Oxford Street, was the address on the card that Denny Cordell had given me. Leaving the Underground at Oxford Circus, I walked to the office entrance of the large corner building that bore this address, and climbed the stairs to the first floor where I walked through a door marked "Regal Zonophone".

A young girl sat behind a desk in the small reception area. She didn't even glance up. After about three minutes I felt I should break the ice.

"I've got an appointment with Denny Cordell," I said, as politely as possible.

She looked up and I could see the reason she had not acknowledged my arrival was that she had been preoccupied with some important filing.

"I'm sorry," I said. "Please finish off your last nail."

She put the emery board down on the desk, and through chewed gum said, "He ain't in."

"But he told me to be here at eleven o'clock."

"He's in the studio with Joe Cocker."

"What time's he due in then?" I asked.

"He ain't."

She returned to her filing and I turned to leave. Amazing,

really, how when one door opens it's nearly always to let you out.

As I opened the door to leave, Tony Visconti walked in.

"Rick," he said. "Come through to my office. Denny's stuck in the studio. He's been in there all night."

I followed him through to his office, where he organised some coffee.

"Do you do many sessions?" he opened up the conversation.

"Not really," I said.

I felt at ease with Tony and took a chance by being a little more open with him than I had been at Olympic Studios. I explained that I was at the Royal College of Music but wasn't really happy there and wanted very much to be a professional musician, eventually making my own music.

Tony looked at me closely for a few seconds.

"You're reaching a time in your life when you've got to make a few important decisions and at the same time take a few chances. There's no doubt in my mind that you have the ability to be very successful. Your style of playing is unlike any other piano player or organist around, and once word gets out about you you're going to be a busy boy in the studio."

I sat listening carefully whilst he continued.

"Having said all that, you must grab the chances whilst they're there. If you're offered sessions and you turn them down because of lectures and lessons then somebody else will get the work, because recordings won't wait until you have a gap in your college schedule."

"My parents will go potty," I said. "They've supported my musical education right from the age of six, even though they could ill afford it, and if I quit now with only a year and a bit to go, they'll be devastated."

"What's the education been for if you can't use it when the opportunity arises?" countered Tony. "Look, Rick. You have a unique style and with the underground music movement breaking through to the surface you are perfectly

Jon Anderson and myself at the Montreux Jazz Festival in 1979.

I received a gold disc in Brazil for *Journey to the Centre of the Earth*.

This picture of the Strawbs shows me in my favourite Afghan coat which was stolen from my Ford Cortina one week after this photograph was taken.

South Harrow Baptist Church

.... MR. R. WAKEMAN .... was

RECEIVED INTO MEMBERSHIP

at the Communion Service on
Sunday 6TH OCTOBER 1968.......

and commended to the prayers and love of the brethren.

........................Minister

" We therefore ought to welcome such, that we may be
fellow-workers with the truth."—3 John, 8 (R.V.).

The card showing the date I was received into membership of South Harrow Baptist Church. (Not to be confused with my baptism which took place a few weeks before.)

Resplendent in glittering robe(!), here I am in 1974.

Stretching between keyboards, I could never do anything ordinary.

I really should have been advertising shampoo here as I seem more intent on looking away from the organ in order to let my hair fall nicely!

The original concert of *Journey to the Centre of the Earth* at the Royal Festival Hall.

Small but unique, the only known photograph of The Spinning Wheel.

More stretching!

Ramon Remedios and myself.

The photo I had done of the band when I recorded *King Arthur*. The lads never forgave m

The finest English Rock Ensemble from 1977.

YES shortly after I joined them in 1971.

Nina and myself. Our favourite picture.

The Showbiz XI at Camberley Town FC before a charity match. I'm the only person I don't recognise.

On the front cover of this magazine is the only known picture of the YES Union line up.

placed to make a name for yourself. For starters, I can give you demo session work here as well as some full sessions to earn you enough to keep the wolf from the door. There's some more work with Jimmy Thomas to do, plus I produce the Strawbs and they always use a session piano player as they don't have one in the band. I've also got Marc Bolan and T-Rex, who I reckon are about to break through, big-time."

My mouth was watering. Tony should have been a politician.

He carried on. "There's another producer here, Gus Dudgeon. He does a lot of production too. I'm sure he'll give you sessions as well. Think about it, Rick, and call me later this week to let me know your decision."

The decision and what I wanted to do were never in question. It was just how to go about it. Time was not on my side and I knew I had to move quickly. Even though I was unaware of it at the time, I had just taken the first really important step in making the decision that was to shape my future in the music industry.

It was Tuesday morning and I had just finished my clarinet lesson with Basil Tchaikof. All three minutes of it.

Basil and I had a good, workable understanding. This had come to fruition almost immediately after my very first, alcohol-ridden lesson with him. For my part, I would subject him to the absolute minimal amount of squeaking and dripping saliva during my allotted half-hour. This was achieved by my playing just one scale and then pleading a shortness of breath. His part would be accepting the weekly excuse, and we would then sit down and have a discussion, usually about music, and then amazingly enough, just as my allotted tutorial time came to an end, I would feel better.

My final lesson with Basil had gone routinely.

"A scale of C please, Mr Wakeman. Two octaves," said Basil.

He shuddered as my saliva intermingled with the appalling-sounding notes of the scale. The impression it gave was that of playing underwater in the bath with the plug just having been pulled out.

I almost hit top C and was actually quite pleased. I had actually never almost hit top C before and this was certainly some personal achievement.

"Bit short of breath," I spluttered.

"Well, we'll give it a rest for a few minutes and have a chat," he said.

I splashed my way over to his desk and sat down.

"How are your other studies going?" he asked.

"I'm actually thinking about leaving," I blurted out.

His eyes lit up and he leaned over the desk.

"Well, we'll be sorry to lose you. I for one enjoy our little chats. Anyway, I expect you'll want to be off now, straight away, so don't let me hold you up. Cheerio, nice to have taught you."

I got the distinct impression that sincerity was not one of Basil Tchaikof's strong points.

"Could I talk to you about it, please, Mr Tchaikof?"

He inwardly groaned, looked at his watch and mentally worked out that it would probably be worth him sitting through twenty minutes of drivel, as the reward at the end of it would be never to see me again.

"Only too pleased to be of help if I can," he lied.

I leaned forward and rambled away about how I was disillusioned with college and didn't want to be a teacher or a classical performer any more.

Whilst I had been waxing lyrical, Basil was obviously getting bored, and after a few minutes picked up his clarinet and started playing some complicated piece for his own amusement. I rather felt he was not wholeheartedly with me in my plight. However, in order to ask me a question he did draw the clarinet away from his mouth.

"What do you want to be then?" he asked.

"A rock musician," I answered.

Together we picked up the pieces of his clarinet from the floor.

"I think the reed's broken, Mr Tchaikof," I said.

He looked at me from a kneeling position.

"Personally, I think you should walk out of these college doors and, without turning round for even a second glance, leave here with just your new career in mind, and never come back. Never ever, not even to pick anything up. Get a friend to bring anything left in your locker to wherever you go. A clean break is what's needed. Right now. This minute. Goodbye."

His voice had become quite high-pitched towards the end of this oratorical advice, almost manic in fact. I swear to this day that I heard a sort of mentally deranged cackling following me down the corridor as I left the room.

My next stop was the offices of Nicholls and Clarke, a large private builders' suppliers in the City of London where my father had risen from the position of office boy, before the war, to that of a very highly respected sales director.

To this day I suspect he had been expecting my visit for some time, because he showed no visible surprise at my unannounced appearance in his office at all, in spite of the fact it was only the second time I had ever been in the building in my entire life.

He took me off to lunch, where he patiently sat listening to all that had happened in my life throughout the past few weeks.

"It's not all going to be plain sailing," he said when I'd finished speaking. "There's no guarantee of regular income with these sessions and the Tony Dee Showband certainly don't earn enough to pay you a living wage, but you seem to have already made your decision and so all I can do as your father is to offer you what moral support I can. Especially with the next, very difficult, stage."

"You mean looking for session work?"

"No, I mean telling your mother you've walked out of college."

It didn't go down at all well.

There were floods of tears, screaming and some of the worst temper tantrums ever witnessed in the Wakeman household. My mother was pretty upset as well.

The major concern for my parents was that of a regular income. They were quite happy for me to live at home, but had no intention of allowing me to loll around the house all day long waiting for work to come in.

My first break in the area of regular work came from the unlikely source of Ronnie Smith.

It was close to Christmas 1968 and Ronnie's organist had, for reasons still unknown to me, walked out. Ronnie was desperate. Christmas was a very busy period. It also transpired that Ronnie's band had now moved to the Top Rank in Reading and there was an extra ten shillings (50p) on offer if I could start the following day.

I jumped at it. After all, it would still leave me free during the day to do whatever sessions came my way.

My first night back was just like old times. Ashley, Rod and Ken were still there, but everyone else was new to me. This time round, though, I was not raw around the gills and therefore not treated like the new boy.

My hair was now touching my collar, I was totally familiar with all the facets of the pop music industry and had, in a relatively short period of time, gained a lot of self-confidence.

Life was pretty good. I lived at home rent-free, although I was hardly ever there, played on as many sessions as were offered during the daytime and worked at the Top Rank in the evening. I purchased an L100 Hammond from the Musical Bargain Centre and did a deal with my father on his two-year-old Ford Cortina. Yes, life was pretty good. Everything fitted in well. Except church on Sunday. That was difficult.

Up until the October of that year, I had hardly missed a Sunday in fifteen years. From Sunday School at the tender age of four, I had worked my way through the church to become a fully qualified Sunday School teacher and a Warrant Officer in the Boys' Brigade. South Harrow Church was a very major part of my life, so much so that on September 18th I was baptised along with my friend Paul Sutton by our minister, the Revd Lorkin.

Two months later my life had changed considerably. I was busy all week doing sessions and generally making myself known around the major studios, and four nights of the week I was working for Ronnie Smith. The other three nights I was out on the town or working as a "sit in" musician in pub bands. Saturday was a very late night at the Top Rank and I rarely got home until five o'clock in the morning. Unable to get up on Sunday mornings through a combination of tiredness and violent hangovers, I found that the morning service at South Harrow quickly fell by the wayside. The evening service was out of the question as I worked on a Sunday night and so, within three months of my being baptised, the church ceased to be any part of my life.

The new year continued in the same vein. Tony Visconti was really good to me as regards work. Everything that required piano or organ on his productions came my way.

Life was pretty good down at Reading, too. I had started going out with a local girl who worked behind the bar, and had also made friends with the chef, who fed me for nothing. Ashley and I continued to make Ronnie's life a misery by doing things with his Hammond that were never mentioned in the manual, and I got a phone call from Gus Dudgeon.

It actually came whilst I was rehearsing at Reading one Thursday afternoon. The manager came over to the bandstand and said there was a phone call for me in his office. I followed him into his room and picked up the phone from his desk.

"Hello," I said.

"Gus Dudgeon here," the voice on the other end replied. "We've not met, but Tony Visconti suggested I call you as he tells me you know how to play the mellotron."

The mellotron was a new keyboard instrument that

attempted to emulate the sound of a violin section by means of prerecorded loop tapes. The machine was fraught with problems. For example, each loop only lasted eight seconds and the more notes you depressed the lower the tuning fell!

I had had considerable experience with one of the first mellotrons to be used in a studio when I had played on an album called *Battersea Power Station*, produced by Tony Visconti for Regal Zonophone. The band was called Junior's Eyes. I had, after much experimenting and serious frustration, discovered a technique of keeping the thing in tune and also of overcoming the problem of notes cutting off.

Gus continued, "Tony has an artist on his roster called David Bowie. He's basically a folk singer and has got this song called 'Space Oddity' which Tony feels he can't produce as David would like and so has asked me to do it. I want to use a mellotron and Tony says you're the man to play it."

He gave me the day and time the session was to take place. I thanked him and returned to rehearsals.

I can remember quite vividly arriving at Trident Studios for the session. The reason was that I was nervous. This was the first session I had ever done where I would know nobody there. I knew none of the other musicians (although they all knew each other) and I had never met the engineer. I had also only spoken to Gus Dudgeon the once when he'd called me at Reading Top Rank to book me for the session.

I was introduced to David Bowie who played us the song on his twelve-string guitar. I remember thinking at the time that it was a tremendous piece of music, really different from anything else about at the time.

I jotted down some chords whilst a backtrack was laid down and then stood at the mellotron to do my bit. Gus basically told me to play where I wanted to and what I felt was right for the track. We did a run-through and Gus declared himself happy. Then we did a take and again Gus declared himself happy. Then Gus gave me a cheque for nine pounds and I went home, via the Ship public house in Wardour Street.

The record was first released on the Philips label as the very first stereo single and is now extremely rare and collectible.

It was not all plain sailing for "Space Oddity", though. Due to a fatal accident involving three American astronauts, the record was not initially released in the USA and was withdrawn in the UK as it was considered by Philips to be in bad taste.

It reappeared on a couple of other labels before finally getting the recognition it deserved around July of 1969. I was thrilled beyond belief as it shot up the charts. I was interviewed by a man called Dan Wooding for the local newspaper, the *Middlesex County Times*. I now found myself in even more demand for sessions and had also become a minor celebrity in my own locality.

The year seemed to be shooting by. I started missing rehearsals at the Top Rank through sheer weight of work. Ronnie had got me doing the functions as well, which I hated and to be honest didn't take at all seriously. I knew that Ronnie was frustrated with me, but I reckoned I now carried the same status as Ashley – irreplaceable.

My sacking was not spectacular. Ronnie just called me into his room, gave me two weeks' notice and told me to get out. It was during those two weeks that I was to witness one of the most spectacular dismissals of a musician in the history of Reading Top Rank.

The whole incident revolved around Terry Cogland, the drummer. Terry had been with Ronnie for years and years and their relationship was stormy, to put it mildly. Terry was a great all-round drummer who needed the regular work to support his wife, son and mortgage. Whilst the money that Ronnie paid was fine for us single guys, it was very difficult for Terry and the other married guys in the band to make ends meet. Terry and Ronnie had regular, quite violent arguments on this subject, with Ronnie always coming out on top by simply saying, "If you don't like it, Terry, then you know what you can do."

And one Wednesday evening at a huge private function for over fifteen hundred people, Terry did it.

At every function Ronnie used to give away two prizes. He would always ask the same two questions to the audience and finish with the same two punch lines.

First, he would ask if anybody had any Green Shield stamps in their pocket or handbag. Everybody would rummage around for a few minutes, before finally some sad person would race up to the stage, waving a strip above their heads, fully expecting to receive some fabulous prize in return for their discovery.

Instead, Ronnie would grab the Green Shield stamps and say, "Thanks very much, I collect them," and then immediately count the band in to continue the dancing whilst everybody laughed at Ronnie's "quick-fire wit".

Terry had heard the same "quick-fire wit" for the last seven years. The novelty had worn off on Terry six years and eleven and a half months earlier.

A little later in the evening, Ronnie would announce that he was about to give away a silver Ronson cigarette lighter to the first person who could come up to the front of the stage and name two film-star dogs.

Ronnie would pull the winner on to the stage, hand them the Green Shield stamps and say, "Here's a dozen Green Shield stamps. You just need to collect another two thousand and you can claim your Ronson lighter."

Guffaws all round and the dancing would continue.

This particular night, Terry cracked. Seven years of Green Shield stamps and wages below the poverty level had obviously pushed him over the edge, and I was one of the privileged few to witness it.

Terry and Ronnie had had a particularly fierce argument before taking the stage for the first set, and both were in really foul moods. During the first interval Terry drank a lot more than usual. During the next break Terry got obliterated.

It was during the third set that Ronnie was do part one of his "giveaway".

It started off innocently enough. Ronnie posed his standard question: "Can somebody bring a strip of Green Shield stamps up to the front of the stage?"

After a few moments a lady appeared, brandishing her stamps. Ronnie pulled her on to the stage. Terry leapt off his drum rostrum, shot down to where Ronnie was standing, grabbed the stamps from the lady and shouted into the microphone, "Thanks ever so much, I collect them."

Everybody roared, especially those on the bandstand. All except Ronnie, that is. Ronnie didn't roar. Ronnie was not amused. He turned and glared at Terry, who was now back behind his drum kit. Terry was grinning like a Cheshire cat.

The band sensed the evening's fun was not yet over. The band sensed correctly.

During the next break, Ronnie read the riot act to Terry. Terry was now paralytic and the frustration of seven years was finally venting itself.

We realised, as Ronnie started the patter about the silver Ronson cigarette lighter, that Terry still had the Green Shield stamps in his pocket. Ronnie also realised this after he had already posed his film-star dogs question. He quickly shouted up to Terry, "Terry, bring the stamps down here, as quick as you can."

Terry arrived at the front of the stage at the same time as a middle-aged lady answered, "Rin Tin Tin and Lassie" into the microphone.

Pushing Ronnie to one side, Terry thrust the strip of Green Shield stamps into her hand and shouted, "You just need a couple of thousand more and you can claim your lighter!"

The place howled. They all thought it was deliberate.

Ronnie had steam coming out of his ears. Terry staggered back to his drum kit. The rest of us were having difficulty playing for laughing, which was not going down at all well with our illustrious bandleader.

He turned and looked up at Terry.

"You're fired," he shouted.

"Pardon, Henry?" slurred Terry.

"You're fired."

Satisfied he had had the last word, Ronnie announced a medley of waltzes and counted us in. It became apparent after a few bars, however, that there were no drums playing. We could hear drums, but they weren't being played. They were being dismantled.

Ronnie looked round in horror.

Terry was now struggling through the brass section with a drum case.

The audience were obviously unsure whether or not this was part of the act. Owing to the fact that the waltz arrangements were now totally impossible to dance to, they surmised it was not a scheduled part of the evening's entertainment and pushed their way towards the front of the stage in order to get a better view of what was going on.

Ronnie did the wisest thing. He announced another break and revolved the stage. Back in the band room he tried to remonstrate with Terry, who was having none of it. He had been fired and was going, there and then.

The final set was performed without drums. It went relatively unnoticed, as most of the people at the function were fast approaching a similar alcoholic state to that of our departing drummer.

Halfway through the set, Terry started taking his packed drum cases out through the dance area to the front entrance. He did not do this quietly and needed several trips in order to get everything out.

The last two cases contained the tom-toms. From the stage it appeared to us that Terry was struggling to carry them. This intrigued us as we knew they weren't heavy. We could only presume that his alcoholic state was now taking its toll physically.

We were, however, incorrect in our assumptions.

Halfway across the dance floor, the cases became too much for Terry and he dropped them. The lids burst open and the contents spilled out all over the floor.

Willing hands rushed to help pick up Terry's tom-toms – and most of Top Rank's cutlery.

I served out my final week's notice and left Ronnie's employ for the last time. I only ever returned to the Top Rank ballroom on one other occasion, which coincidentally was the same week as my picture appeared on the front of *Melody Maker*, with the headline "Tomorrow's Superstar".

Ashley had had it photocopied, enlarged and stuck to Ronnie Smith's door with a further sign pinned above it which read: "Ronnie Smith sacked this man twice. This could be you."

7

Home and away

I was now as good as unemployed. True, there were a few sessions coming in, but with no guaranteed regular income, the lifestyle to which I had grown accustomed disappeared fast.

It wasn't that I had earned a lot, it was just that the only expense I had ever had was running my car. I slept and ate at either my parents' or my girlfriend's parents' house and was still living rent-free at home. The lifestyle to which I had grown accustomed mainly revolved around drinking large quantities of alcohol through to the early hours of the morning.

To complicate matters, I had got engaged to Ros Woolford, the girl behind the bar at the Top Rank. It had not gone down well with my parents, who thought I had gone stark raving mad. I was twenty and all my mates had got married, so it seemed the natural thing to do to join the club.

My father pointed out one or two possible flaws in my marital plans.

"You've got no job, no work on the horizon, nowhere to live and no money."

I stood up to him and gave him back as good as he gave me.

"Yeah, I hear what you're saying, but now give me one good reason why I shouldn't get married."

He shook his head in an exasperated fashion, which at the time I read as his way of admitting defeat. In later years, I reread that particular exasperated head-shaking episode as a visual way of his saying, "I despair of you, you drunken, immature, brainless waste of space."

I realised I needed regular income if I was going to get married, and so I scoured the classified ads in the back of the *Melody Maker*, looking for work. There were quite a few that wanted organists and so I spent the morning on the phone, seeing what there was going.

Most of them were bands that were just starting; all had "promises" of huge record contracts.

"Hi, man. We're called the Perfumed Sewerage. We're musically a heavy blend of Vanilla Fudge and Cilla Black. Every major wants to sign us, man."

"How long have you been together?"

"A week."

I was just on the verge of giving up when I came to an advertisement which simply read:

Wanted. Competent organist. Reading essential. £40 per week.

I immediately thought that it must be a misprint. The average wage was only around the twenty-five pound a week mark and musicians didn't earn that kind of money, or so I thought.

The phone was answered by a guy called Peter Sills, who turned out to be the guitarist and was putting a band together for a residency. He couldn't tell me much more than that, except that the rest of the band had already been assembled and the organist was the last position he had to fill. There was also an organ supplied for use by the successful applicant. The music would be mainly cover versions of the current hits of the day, although a few standards would also be included.

The auditions were to be held from midday onwards at the Green Gate pub in Ilford, Essex.

I got there about a quarter to twelve and sat in a large ballroom with about thirty other guys who, one by one, were called up on stage to play with the band, which consisted of a drummer, bass player, guitarist and singer. They were all excellent musicians and sounded very tight. I was about number twenty-five on the list to play, so I went to the bar with the intention of also becoming very tight.

My name was finally called out and I climbed on stage. The organ was a new Lowrey, which was not my favourite make but a very usable machine just the same. They thrust a piece of current pop music in front of me and we played it. Then we played the Beatles' "Norwegian Wood", and then Peter told me I started a week on Monday at the Greyhound pub in Chadwell Heath, and yes, it was forty pounds a week.

We worked every night and Sunday lunchtimes and it was great fun. It was packed every night and the band was very professional and very popular. The commuting from my parents' house to Ilford every day wasn't too bad, but at the weekends when I picked up Ros from Reading, it meant a round trip of a couple of hundred miles for each day.

My employer was a man called Bob Wheatley. He was a very clever, astute man who realised that people wanted good-quality entertainment without having to lay out West End prices. He also realised that a lot of the pubs in east London and Essex were very large and a lot of them had huge function rooms which remained unused for most of the year. The biggest brewery chain in this area was Charrington's, and Bob did a deal with them where he took over the function rooms and ballrooms and put a resident band in each one. There was no charge for admission, but a few pence were added to all the drink prices.

Within a year the Charrington pubs were called Wheatley Taverns.

Bob was a "hands on" man and visited each of his pubs every night at closing time to check on business.

The Greyhound at Chadwell Heath, with our band, the Spinning Wheel, became the most popular pub in the area, and I loved every minute of it.

I found a flat near by in Clarendon Road, Ilford, and I signed a contract which allowed me to move in at the end of March 1970, shortly before Ros and I were to be married at a church in Reading.

Sessions had started to pick up, and I was doing a lot of BBC work for Radio One programmes such as *The Jimmy Young Show*. Tony Visconti had also introduced me to the Strawbs and I played organ on their album *Dragonfly*. They invited me to play with them on their appearances on Radio Two's *Folk on Friday* programme.

Late in February, they invited me to join the band full time and tour with them.

At that time they were still very much a folk band, with a line-up consisting of two acoustic guitars played by the band's founders, Dave Cousins and Tony Hooper, plus an alcoholic Scottish string-bass player and a female cellist.

They were very popular around the folk clubs, and in spite of the fact that I was not particularly fond of folk music I found Dave Cousins' compositions really enjoyable to play and his lyrics nothing short of outstanding. Dave and I became firm friends and we discussed at length the idea of turning Strawbs into the first folk-rock band.

In reality it was not going to be simple for me to join the Strawbs. For starters, I had a two-year contract with Bob Wheatley. Secondly, the Strawbs were only able to pay twenty pounds a week. The big plus, though, was that they wanted me to start the week after I was getting married by playing for a week with them in Paris, and I could bring Ros with me as a working honeymoon. That clinched it for me, and I arranged an appointment to see Bob Wheatley at his private office.

"You're telling me that you want to join this folk band called the Strawbs, are willing to take a massive drop in

wages and want to forget our contract. Is that correct?"
said Bob after I had told him the situation and asked if I
could hand in a month's notice.

I nodded.

"What's the name of the Strawbs' management?" Bob
asked. "And give me their telephone number."

I gave him the necessary information and immediately he
dialled the given number and spoke to Mike Dolan, the
Strawbs' manager.

I could only hear one side of the conversation but felt
things were not going my way, as Bob was continually saying,
"That's as may be, but the fact is he has a contract with me
that has another year and a half to run."

Finally he replaced the receiver.

"I do not understand why anybody, especially somebody
who's about to get married, wants to leave a secure job and
take half wages in an unknown folk band. Do you like folk
music that much?"

"Actually, I don't really like folk music at all."

"I'm intrigued, then. You've got two minutes to convince
me to tear your contract up. Off you go."

I did my best to explain to him that, with my help, Dave
Cousins wanted to change Strawbs' image by taking it out
of the folk clubs and then turn it into one of the first true
folk-rock bands, and that for my part I really felt I could
play a big role in this transformation.

Bob looked across his desk at me.

"You're mental," he said, and tore up the contract.

"Work with the Spinning Wheel until the end of April,
which will give them time to sort out a replacement. Oh,
and good luck. I think you're going to need it."

I didn't see Bob Wheatley for another three years. I was
actually at a testimonial dinner at the Grosvenor House in
London for a West Ham footballer, and towards the end
of the evening, the late, great former captain of England,
Bobby Moore, came over to my table. My love of soccer was

by this time legendary, and I had many friends in football, Bobby being amongst them.

I proudly introduced Bobby around my table, and then he asked me if I would go over to his table as there were some Yes fans there who would like to meet me.

By now, Yes had had two massively successful albums and I had had my first solo success as well, with *The Six Wives of Henry VIII*. I was a regular on the front cover of music magazines and was up there in the forefront of progressive rock.

I arrived at Bobby's table. The men stood up one by one and I was introduced to each of them. Finally, the man directly in front of me, with his back towards me, turned round with a smile on his face and stood up. It was Bob Wheatley.

He stood by my side, put his arm round me and addressed the table.

"Rick," he said, "you've done pretty well for yourself in the last three years. How many records have you sold?"

"Not exactly sure," I replied, "but somewhere around the five million mark."

"And what size of audience do you get these days?"

I was not sure where all this questioning was leading, but I went along with it anyway.

"Well, in America, about twenty thousand people a night."

Bob turned his attention to the puzzled throng around the table.

"Ladies and gentlemen, I have been highly successful in every one of my business exploits, especially those involving entertainment. I also run things absolutely by the book and have rock-hard contracts with everyone who works for me. This man here signed a two-year contract with me which I tore up with a year and a half of it still to run because I thought he was mental. Watching his progress over the last three years has made me realise that I was the one who was mental!

"The least you can do now, Rick," he continued, "is to

buy me a drink. In fact you can buy the whole table a drink!"

I often thought in later years what a tremendous manager Bob Wheatley would have made.

After leaving Bob's office I immediately called Arnakata Music, who were Strawbs' management, to tell them that I was now free to join the band as from the end of April. It was agreed that I would rehearse with them during the daytime whilst still working in the evenings with the Spinning Wheel.

Ros and I moved into the flat in Clarendon Road and life changed. Things like bills came flying through the letter-box. I didn't like them. Bills like rates, electricity, gas, water. I suddenly realised that living wasn't free. I also realised very quickly that my twenty pounds a week from Strawbs was not going to be sufficient to survive. Ros had a job which brought in eight pounds a week, but my father's warnings as to the cost of getting married and supporting a wife now suddenly became very real.

Financial difficulties were overshadowed, though, by the thrill of being part of a band. Rehearsals went well and privately Dave Cousins told me of his plans for the band after the Paris trip was over. It involved replacing the string-bass player with an electric-bass player and introducing my Hammond organ into the line-up, instead of my just playing piano.

I was very excited and exactly one day after my last appearance at the Greyhound in Chadwell Heath, I was boarding the ferry at Dover, bound for Calais.

We arrived in Paris in the early hours of the morning and eventually found ourselves outside this very seedy back-street hotel.

Because Tony Hooper was the most respectable-looking of all of us, he did the checking in. By this time my hair was getting very long and Dave, with his beard and fairly long hair, frightened normal people. Nobody could understand the Scottish double-bass player, who was drunk most of the time anyway, and so Tony's position as internal tour manager was thrust upon him more by necessity than anything else.

It had been a long day and so Ros went to bed whilst I joined the other lads in the bar, which conveniently stayed open all night, for a band meeting. This was not a popular marital decision and was even less popular at the time as it was, after all, our honeymoon, but band meetings were very important. Vital issues were always discussed, such as "Whose round is it next?" and "Will that funny-looking green drink in that bottle make me violently sick?"

Nobody ever ate breakfast, so we ended up going directly from the bar to the venue at about nine o'clock in the morning. We had to stop a couple of times on the way, as our Scottish bass player insisted on hanging his head over various bridges that crossed the River Seine, due to his discovery that the funny-looking green drink did in fact make you violently sick.

The venue was outrageous. It was a circus tent! Some mad Frenchman had decided to put on a rock and roll circus.

The basic idea was to have all the usual circus acts, but instead of having the normal run-of-the-mill circus music with a circus band, the artistes and animals would perform to live rock bands.

The promoter had chosen various groups whose music he felt suited particular acts. For example, we were to play for the child jugglers, the tightrope walker and the man who fell off tables. The Crazy World of Arthur Brown were to perform whilst the lion tamer did his bit and Heavy Jelly were to accompany the acrobats and horse-riders.

Whilst on paper the idea may have looked magnificent, in reality it was fraught with difficulties. For starters, on the posters the promoter had got all the bands' names completely wrong. We were "Les Strobes," there was "The Amazing World of Andy Bown" and "Hovvy Jolly." The bands were not pleased about this, but it was too late to do anything about it as all the posters had already been printed and displayed all over Paris.

Heavy Jelly went home after the first day as they frightened the horses. Arthur Brown split his trousers during his opening number and was taken away by the French authorities. Two bands of a much gentler nature appeared in their place.

Our three pieces were instantly reduced to two when the man who fell off tables fell off and broke his leg, but we were rewarded by being offered the chance to play whilst the lion tamer did his act. This only lasted a couple of days, though, as the lion tamer used to have to literally drag the lion into the ring because it was so heavily drugged; after two days he was also taken away by the French authorities.

The child jugglers were awful, they dropped more than they caught, and the tightrope was so slack that by the time the tightrope walker had reached the middle he was only eighteen inches off the ground.

The major problem was the audience. Basically, there wasn't one. Half a dozen people turned up, at most. It became very obvious to us all that someone was losing a lot of money and that someone was also likely to be the person who was meant to pay us and our hotel bill as well. Careful investigation gleaned the information that our hotel bills hadn't as yet been paid but were due to be settled the following week, on the day we were to leave, by the promoter.

To give the promoter his due, he did make one final effort to get publicity for the rock and roll circus. He somehow managed to get Salvador Dali to make an appearance, which he hoped would give credibility to the event. There was one major flaw in this plan, and that was that I had no idea who Salvador Dali was and that nobody warned me he was going to appear on stage in the middle of my piano solo.

I had only one solo to play and I looked forward to it every night. The fact that nobody was there to hear it was irrelevant, it was my solo and my adrenalin level rose accordingly.

I was halfway through it when suddenly from nowhere this tall, elderly man, with the most ludicrous moustache I had ever seen, appeared standing next to the electric piano that I was playing, banging the top of it with his walking-stick. I quite naturally deduced that this was a man who had escaped from a local lunatic asylum and was potentially dangerous. More importantly, he was wrecking my solo, so I made a decisive move. I pushed him off the stage.

Organisers rushed to pick him up and he was dragged away, ranting and raving, whilst making threatening gestures at me with his stick.

I finished my solo and Dave wandered over to me.

"Do you know who that was?" he asked.

"Some drunk ruining my solo," I answered.

"That was Salvador Dali."

"Is he a friend of yours, then?" I asked. I was beginning to get the impression that I had not perhaps acted in quite the right way.

"He's Spain's most famous living artist and you've just tried to kill him."

We made the front pages of most of the following day's newspapers. At least, Salvador Dali did. His picture was very prominent on most of the front pages which showed him waving his stick about in obvious displeasure. They all spelt my name incorrectly, as well as the word "hooligan" which I suppose does not translate literally into French.

The circus closed two days later after the promoter went missing. Quietly collecting our belongings from the hotel, we left for Calais, reassuring the proprietor that somebody from the promoter's office would be along very soon to sort out all the bills. I have a nasty suspicion that they could still be waiting.

We returned to England and started rehearsals with a new line-up. Richard "Hud" Hudson and John Ford joined the band from Elmer Gantry's Velvet Opera. John played bass and Hud played congas and percussion as well as the sitar. I introduced my Hammond organ to the line-up and Dave bought himself an electric guitar to play, as well as his acoustics.

Dave had written a new piece entitled "The Antique Suite" which we learned and rehearsed at the same time as re-arranging a lot of the old Strawbs numbers. The gig book was quite full, mostly with folk club appearances, but this soon started to change as basically the folk clubs weren't ready for us. They certainly weren't ready for what we were now doing with the new line-up, and they found it difficult to cope with things like Dave coming to the end of one of his beautiful lyrics, as in the song "My Love is Like a Rose", and then watching me tip the Hammond on to its side and play it with a paint roller.

We quickly moved on to the university circuit, which was much better suited to what we were doing.

Our popularity was growing fast, but perhaps not as fast as we all thought. This was highlighted very late one night at the Blue Boar service station on the M1 where we had stopped on the way home from a gig for a bite to eat.

The Blue Boar is very much a part of rock legend. It was the service station around the Coventry/Northampton region on the motorway where every band stopped on their way home from gigs. It was pretty rough and would only serve food on paper plates and with plastic knives and forks. In those days, nobody would go anywhere near it who wasn't either in a band, a Hell's Angel or just escaped from prison.

I stood in the self-service queue and piled some sausage, chips and beans on to my paper plate, like everybody else hoping I could get it to the table before it became soggy and collapsed.

I got to the end of the line where a young girl sat behind the cash register, looking thoroughly bored.

She looked at my plate and then up at me. Her eyes opened wide and her jaw dropped.

"It's you, isn't it?" She entered the first stages of mild hysteria.

"It is, isn't it?" She entered the second stage immediately.

I tried to act as cool as possible. People at the tables were starting to sit up and take notice.

"I knew as soon as I saw you that it was you." She was now totally hysterical.

I looked along at the rest of the band behind me and then beyond at other people in the queue and, shrugging my shoulders and gesticulating wildly with my arms, gave the best impression that I could muster of a famous rock star in the presence of a totally adoring female fan. I looked around at those seated at tables, who had stopped eating and were staring in my direction. I gave them the "knowing smile" in return.

The young girl turned in her chair and slid back the window that separated her from those working in the kitchen. She shouted through the aperture.

"Hey, girls! Look who's here."

Half a dozen faces appeared through the gap.

"It's Jethro Tull," she said and turned and beamed at me.

"Er, we're not actually Jethro Tull," I said quietly, hoping that nobody else apart from her could hear me.

"Well, who are you then?" she said, making sure that everybody could hear her.

"The Strawbs," I said.

"Never heard of you." She looked down at my plate, which had now dissolved, and then at my food, which had slid on to the plastic tray. "That's sausage, chips and beans and a mug of coffee. Eight and six [42½p]."

It was a long walk to the table through a sea of grinning faces.

I realised we were still a very long way from stardom.

8

Changes

We had started to get good reviews in most of the major music papers, who at the same time were also saying some kind things about my playing. *Melody Maker*, in particular, reviewed us regularly in their "Caught In The Act" section, which, it has to be said, was not always as honest as the readers were led to believe.

Because the gig scene was so strong at the beginning of the seventies, bands were permanently on the road. Magazines couldn't afford to send journalists all over the country and so would use freelance writers in local towns wherever possible. Some of them didn't know a hatchet from a crotchet. Some of them are now editors of major music magazines.

I well remember a gig we were doing in Dundee. We knew it was going to be reviewed by *Melody Maker* but we didn't know by whom. About an hour before we were due on stage, there was a knock on the dressing-room door and an elderly gentleman asked if he could speak to somebody from the Strawbs. The lads were all very busy drinking and all pointed at me. Cries of "He's your man" and "He'll tell you anything you want to know" filled the air.

Before I knew what was happening, I found myself alone with this stranger, who took out a notebook from his pocket.

"I've been asked to review the concert tonight," he began tentatively, "and I was hoping somebody could help me out before I go and pick my wife up. We're going to the cinema tonight. She likes the cinema. We don't get out much these days, you know."

I thought it a good idea to try and interrupt him before he got into full flow about his marital likes and dislikes.

"How can you go to the cinema and review our concert at the same time?" I thought this a reasonable question to start with.

"Oh, I'm not coming to the concert," he said. "I don't like modern music very much. I don't like it at all, to be honest. Not very tuneful, you know, and it gives me a headache."

"How come you're reviewing the show, then?" This seemed a reasonable follow-up question.

"Well, I was contacted a while back by the editor of *Melody Maker* who offered me twenty pounds every time I did a review for them. Well, that's more than I make in a week normally, and so I jumped at the chance. I never actually go to any shows, though, I just meet somebody from the band, they tell me the set list and give me a brief description of what they consider to be the highlights of the show, and I write the review up and take the wife out for the night."

I sat there, flabbergasted.

He continued, "I don't always get to meet the group. Sometimes I only get to see a roadie. I've reviewed all the top bands, you know, the Who, Black Sabbath, Jeffrey Tell."

"Jethro Tull," I corrected him.

"Oh, I wondered why they never used that review."

Hud walked into the dressing-room.

"This gentleman needs a bit of help with the review," I said. "Can we assist him, do you think, Hud?"

Hud felt we certainly could and after getting the old boy completely plastered and very happy, we sent him off on his way.

The review from Dundee was sensational.

The management now decided that we should play a major London venue and record it live at the same time. The Queen Elizabeth Hall was booked for July 11th 1971, and Tony Visconti was brought in to record and produce the LP from the performance.

By the time July arrived, we had the show off to a fine art. If anything, we peaked the night before the Queen Elizabeth Hall when we played at Exeter University, but to everybody's relief the big day went without a hitch and the sell-out crowd gave us a tremendous reception. Backstage afterwards, we were told by the management that the national press were in and we could expect reviews in *The Times*, the *Guardian* and the *Financial Times*.

The following morning, I bought all three papers. All three carried reviews and all three were tremendous. They also each singled me out for a special mention, which was fantastic. From then on, things took a giant leap forward, especially when the very next issue of *Melody Maker* put a picture of me on the front page along with the headline, "Tomorrow's Superstar".

Arnakata Music had been inundated with requests for interviews and the leading rock public relations man, Tony Brainsby, was taken on board to handle the situation.

I spoke to anybody and everybody over the next couple of months. Teenybop magazines, tabloids, the music press, local newspapers and even World Service radio. If anybody wanted to interview to me, I was there. Invariably over a drink.

My drinking reputation was actually growing as fast as my musical one, but this didn't worry me at all. On the contrary, I got more press because of it. Most of the reporters enjoyed a drink or two, and invariably when the interview was over we would end up going out on a serious drinking session and subsequently become good friends.

In spite of the fact that the live album from the Queen Elizabeth Hall, entitled *Just a Collection of Antiques and Curios*, got to number twenty-nine in the album charts, I was still only earning twenty pounds a week with Strawbs and was unable to supplement my income by doing sessions, as we were permanently on the road. I was always late with the rent and my landlady, Mrs Cleary, was fast losing patience with me. Just before Christmas, she told me she wanted us out by the end of March when our lease expired.

I was devastated. With an income of twenty pounds a week, and outgoings probably closer to thirty, finding somewhere to live was not going to be easy.

I talked the situation over with my father, who said it was a shame that I wasn't in a position to take out a mortgage, as he felt that there would never be a better time to get on the house-ownership ladder. He asked me how much I had been able to save throughout the year. I answered by going into great lengths as to the rising cost of equipment, travel and self-promotion.

He translated this into English. "You've got nothing saved, then."

"Not exactly, Dad," I replied.

"Well, you're going to have to sort something out pretty quick, my son, or else you're going to be homeless."

It certainly was a dilemma that I could see no answer to. My father could see that very clearly but did his best to paint the options for me.

"I don't know whether or not you are aware of it, but all you need as a deposit these days on a house costing between four and five thousand is about five hundred pounds. Is there no way you can raise that from somewhere? I happen to know of a lovely two-bedroomed terraced house in West Harrow that is about to come on the market for about four and a half thousand, which I'm sure would be perfect for you; but whatever you do, you're going to have to move fast because it takes about three months to get a mortgage organised with all the necessary paperwork, and that, my son, is all you've got."

I discussed the situation with the Strawbs' management. I opened proceedings with a relatively pointless question. "Is there any chance of a rise over the next three months, and if there is, can I have some of it in advance, please?"

I was given the standard management answer.

"Sit down, Rick. Now, as you are very well aware, the band is going through a potential growth period which involves careful investment of all performance and royalty income in order to alleviate any future shortfall in cash flow that may occur."

That's management-speak for "No".

I explained to them my dilemma and said that I would probably have to quit the band and go back to doing sessions in order to earn enough money to rent somewhere to live.

Mike Dolan leaned across his desk.

"I have an idea that might solve your problem. I have an involvement with a film that's going to be shot early in the new year and I also have some input into the soundtrack production. I'm sure I could guarantee you the job of composing the music and get you a fee of about five hundred pounds for writing it. Leave it with me for a couple of days and I'll see what I can pull together."

Two days later it was all sorted out, or so the management led me to believe. The film job was mine, with an advance of five hundred pounds to be paid at the end of March 1971. In retrospect, I'm now convinced that there was never any film and I was just told what they wanted me to hear in order to stop me leaving the band and returning to session work. Unwittingly, though, whatever the motive, they had done me a great favour.

Armed with the knowledge that I would shortly have access to the deposit on a house, I proceeded with the purchase of the property my father had told me about. I organised a mortgage and gave my lawyer a post-dated cheque for five hundred pounds to cover the deposit, which would be presented to my bank on the day that the contracts were due to be exchanged.

One month before the day of completion, the Strawbs' management informed me that the film had been cancelled.

I was devastated. I had less than a pound in the bank and in under a month the Westminster Bank at South Ealing would have one of my cheques presented to them for five hundred pounds.

There was no way out but to own up and tell the truth to all concerned with the house purchase. My first telephone call was to the bank.

I made an appointment for that same afternoon to see Mr Williams, the bank manager, whom I had never met before. People who never had more than three pounds in their account never got to meet bank managers.

I was not looking forward to this meeting. However many ways I rehearsed what I was going to say, there was no disguising my problem. I had written a cheque out for at least five hundred times more money than I had in my account.

Mr Williams was a tall, elegant man in his late fifties. I was ushered into his oak-panelled office, where he rose from behind his desk and obviously struggled to get over the shock of seeing me for the first time. I instantly realised that my appearance was not one that he was used to in the banking world.

"Sit down, Mr Wakeman." He motioned to a chair. "Now, what can I do for you?"

I spent the next five minutes explaining the situation as eloquently as possible. I left nothing out, going through everything that had happened in my short career and also the advice given to me by my father.

Mr Williams sat quietly until I finally ground to a halt.

"You'll still be liable for solicitor's fees, I expect," he said. "Have you any idea how much they will be?"

I'd forgotten all about them.

"Not exactly, sir. I think around about a hundred pounds."

He opened a folder in front of him.

"Let's have a look at where your account stands at the moment," he said.

He studied the page in front of him and then spoke, without looking up.

"You have a credit of eighteen shillings and sixpence [92^1/$_2$p]."

He looked up and continued speaking.

"What do you think your musical prospects are for the coming year, Mr Wakeman? Could you supplement your income at all by doing some more of these sessions you told me about, playing on other people's records?"

I said that I honestly didn't know, but felt very positive about my career.

"I'm going to clear your cheque when it arrives," said Mr Williams.

I was totally at a loss for words.

"I think your father is spot on with his assessment of the housing market. It has been stagnant for too long and I agree with him that prices will start to soar within a couple of years. I'm going to give you a six hundred and fifty pound overdraft facility to cover the mortgage deposit and your legal fees. Please let me have all the details of the property so that I can draw up the necessary paperwork."

He rose from behind his desk and showed me to the door.

One month later I exchanged contracts and moved into the house in Vaughan Road, West Harrow.

From the moment that I walked out of Mr Williams' office, sessions started to pour in. They came at a good time for me as Dave was busy working on new material for the forthcoming album, and so gigs were at a minimum.

After about a month, Strawbs were ready to go into the studio to produce our second album since I'd joined, and that's where the first differences of opinion really arose in the ranks. Hud and John were also very good writers, but of a totally different style from Dave, and I felt that the material put forward for the album was too diverse. With the exception of "The Shepherd's Song" and "A Glimpse of Heaven", I found it difficult to offer much to the music. If the truth be known, I didn't put anywhere near as much work into the album as I should have done.

I started taking as many sessions as I could whilst not working in the studio on the Strawbs album. The diary became more and more packed with work and the Strawbs album took second place in my ever-increasing workload.

I was taking at least two sessions a day, and more whenever possible. This certainly caused friction in the band, who were having to schedule my keyboard contributions around my outside work. Having said this, I was really pleased with my contribution to some of the tracks, notably "Sheep", "A Glimpse of Heaven", "The Shepherd's Song" and "The Hangman and the Papist". The album was given the title *From The Witchwood* and had mixed reviews.

I was fast realising that I would never be able to keep up the mortgage payments on a house, plus all the bills that went along with home ownership, on a Strawbs wage of twenty pounds a week. The management made it clear that there was no sign of any pay rise on the horizon, which was fast forcing my hand towards the "leaving" direction regarding a decision as to whether or not I would be able to afford to continue in the band.

During 1971 I had the great pleasure of working in the studio with some of the greatest writers, performers and producers around. The list included artists from all areas of the industry, and I played on such diverse recordings as those by Cilla Black, Lou Reed, Black Sabbath, Cat Stevens (including his legendary version of "Morning Has Broken"), David Bowie, Elton John, Mary Hopkin, Al Stewart, Clive Dunn and Marc Bolan, to name but a few.

The most memorable has to be that of the recording of the *Hunky Dory* album by David Bowie.

David had invited me round to his house in Beckenham, which I nicknamed Beckenham Palace as it was the biggest house I had ever seen. After he had proudly showed off his new son, Zowie, we relaxed in the huge lounge and David took his twelve-string guitar out of its case.

"I'm going to play you some songs that I've written for the new album," he began, "and I want you to learn them on the piano and then play them back to me in your own style. I really want to come at this album from a piano angle instead of that of the guitar."

He then proceeded to play the finest selection of songs I have ever heard in one sitting in my entire life. I doubt whether anybody will ever experience such a wonderfully unique evening as I had the pleasure of that night.

I had been given the honour of hearing tracks like "Life on Mars" and "Changes" in their raw brilliance. I couldn't wait to get into the studio to record them.

The first day of recording at Trident Studios in London was one of the most bizarre in my session career. "Life on Mars" was the first backtrack to record and it became pretty obvious after a few run-throughs that David's band hadn't learned the piece. After about an hour and a half of "going nowhere", David came down the stairs into the studio and addressed the band.

"You've had two weeks to learn the material for this album. It's obvious you've been wasting valuable rehearsal time. Now you're wasting my time, Tony's time and," he looked over at where I was sitting at the piano, "Rick's time."

I sat looking down at the piano keys, trying to appear as inconspicuous as possible, while the roasting continued.

"You can pack all your gear up and go back to the house and start rehearsing right now. You've got one week to learn the music or I'll replace every single one of you."

He looked over at me.

"I'm sorry about this, Rick. Could you please go up to the control room and have a word with Tony?"

Tony was sitting behind the control desk as I walked through the door. He basically reiterated what David had said and asked if I could possibly reschedule myself to fit the sessions in the following week. I recall it not being too much of a problem, and one week later found myself sitting back at the piano in Trident Studios with an incredibly well-rehearsed band.

*　　　*　　　*

July 1971 brought about perhaps one of the most difficult musical decisions I have ever had to make and probably ever will.

I had already decided to quit Strawbs purely for financial reasons and to return to doing sessions full time where I knew I could make four times as much money on a regular basis. Then came the two telephone calls that were to shape the next stage of my musical career.

The first came from David Bowie. He asked me to meet him that evening at a club in Hampstead to discuss a proposition he had for me.

David was doing a surprise performance at the club with just himself and Mick Ronson on guitar. David was dressed in the most wild outfit I had ever seen, which included giant blue feathers protruding from a Tiller-girl style headdress.

After David's performance, which completely freaked the audience out, he came and sat down with me at a private table near the bar.

"I'm forming a band which I'm going to call 'Spiders from Mars'," he began, "and I'm going to become Ziggy Stardust. I want you to be part of the band and be responsible for the arrangements as well. You can have a lot of freedom and the money will be good as my management are in the middle of negotiating for an album and a world tour."

I was flattered beyond belief. Here was an opportunity to stay out on the road, which I really enjoyed, and earn enough to pay the mortgage at the same time! David told me to spend a couple of days thinking about it and then to call him. I told David there and then that it sounded great and I really fancied the whole idea, but David insisted I took my time over the decision.

The following night, or three o'clock in the morning to be precise, the telephone rang with the other call. This one was from Chris Squire of Yes.

We had met once before when Strawbs had supported Yes at a gig in Hull. I remember staying to hear their set and being intrigued by their sound, which was totally different from anything else around at the time. They also looked different, almost wrong in fact.

Most bands at that time had lead singers who were tall and had deep throaty voices. Jon Anderson was diminutive and had a pure adult falsetto. Bass players, with the exception of John Entwhistle of the Who, were pretty much backroom boys. Not so Chris Squire, whose treble-sounding bass played as melodic bass lines as I had ever heard. Bill Bruford seemed very composed on the drums as against the usual drummer who normally sat in a pile of sweat, and Steve Howe was the first guitarist I had heard for a long time that didn't sound like Eric Clapton. Perhaps the only area that came across as standard was that of Tony Kaye on the organ, who in fairness was not given a leading role within the music.

To this day I vividly remember the opening of the conversation with Chris. I had not got home from a late session until about two o'clock that morning and had to be up at seven to get into London. I was in a deep sleep when the phone rang.

I picked up the phone and struggled to pull myself up into a sitting position.

"Hello," I ventured.

"Oh, hello, this is Chris Squire. We have met once before, up in Hull if you remember. Anyway, we've just returned today from our first American tour and we've come to the conclusion that we want to move more into orchestral keyboards and, having read some of your interviews and heard you play, feel that you are the perfect musician to help us both achieve our joint aims. What do you think?"

"What time is it?"

"Er, ten past three."

"I've got to be up at seven."

"Shall I call you back tomorrow, then?"

"Please."

And that ended the conversation.

I got back home the following day about six o'clock in the evening. There were four messages from Chris Squire to call him and also a couple from the manager of Yes, Brian Lane.

I spoke to Chris, who said that Brian wanted to arrange a meeting up at their offices, in South Street in the heart of Mayfair. I called Brian first thing the following morning and a meeting was set up at which I met up with both Jon and Chris. We arranged to have a rehearsal the next day to see if we fitted in together. I felt there was nothing to lose by this and arrived at the rehearsal room at the duly arranged time.

At that rehearsal we pretty much composed "Round-about" and "Heart of the Sunrise". I was over the moon. The standard of musicianship was phenomenal and I knew this band wanted to go places, and I wanted to go with them.

I arrived back home thinking about how I was going to tell Strawbs what I wanted to do, and found myself with another problem awaiting my return. It came in the form of a message from David Bowie's office, asking for confirmation that I would be fronting Spiders from Mars.

I spent the evening in the Apollo public house at the end of the road trying to decide what to do about my dilemmas. First I had to choose between Yes and Bowie. I chose Yes, simply because I would be an equal member of the band with equal opportunities, plus the fact that the music we had come up with at that day's rehearsal was stupendous. With David, I would always be a member of his band and much as I loved working with him I realised that there was only so far I could go along that route. The next day I phoned David and told him personally of my decision. He wished me much success and we have remained friends ever since. There is no doubt that I learned much from working with him and thoroughly enjoyed reminiscing with him the last time we worked together, on *Absolute Beginners*.

I performed for the last time with Strawbs at a BBC live radio recording for *The John Peel Show* in the last week of

July. It was a strange feeling, watching my Hammond organ being loaded into the Yes van that had come to the studio to pick my gear up after the show was over. I confess I shed a few tears in the car as I drove home after shaking hands with Dave, Tony, Hud and John for the last time.

I woke up two days later to my second front cover of *Melody Maker* in twelve months. This time the headline above the picture simply read, "Wakeman Joins Yes".

9

Give and take

After a few weeks of pretty intense rehearsals we were ready to go into Advision Studios to record the now legendary *Fragile* album. Strangely enough, I knew from the moment we started recording that it was going to be something special, as neither the record company nor the management remotely understood what we were doing!

With Eddie Offord at the mixing desk, between us we worked literally twenty-four hours a day. The album was completed inside six weeks and the immediate buzz was tremendous.

The well-known individualist artist Roger Dean had been brought in to design a cover, and he became very involved with us over the next few years in the design of stage sets as well as album covers.

The album shot straight into the top ten of the album chart and we embarked on a nationwide tour. With wages of fifty pounds a week coming in from Yes I was financially sound as regards my outgoings, and so was able to wind down all my session activities to concentrate solely on Yes.

It was a wonderful period. I was delighted to see Strawbs produce a hit single, "Part of the Union" and a hit album, *Bursting at the Seams*, so it looked as though everything had worked out really well for all concerned. To cap it all, Ros was expecting our first child in February.

An American tour had been booked for the end of the year and I was very excited at the prospect of crossing the Atlantic to play for the first time. We arrived in Los Angeles where we initially performed for five nights at the Whisky-a-Go-Go Club on Sunset Boulevard. The *Fragile* album had yet to be released in America and so the set was mainly made up of material from *The Yes Album*, which although then not a big-selling album had at least been released over there. The pieces we included from *Fragile* were "Heart of the Sunrise" and "Roundabout".

For the next six weeks we played third and fourth on the bill to such acts as Ten Years After and Edgar Winter, in huge indoor arenas capable of holding over twenty thousand people. It has to be said that there were never twenty thousand people in the building when we went on stage, which was usually around about seven o'clock. We were allotted twenty-five minutes to play on whatever stage space the headline act would allow us, which was never very much. The headline act would set all their gear up first, with strict instructions that it was not to be moved. They would also use up most of the inputs on the mixing desk. The other bands on the bill would then have to fight for space. For us, being the bottom of the bill virtually meant playing on each other's shoulders!

This created many problems for me, as on the UK tour I had introduced to the keyboard world the idea of balancing keyboards one on top of the other and then surrounding myself with them. On this tour, that was particularly difficult, and to this day I don't know how on earth the road crew got my equipment on stage.

After the first few shows I was pretty downcast. During most of our twenty-five minutes of playing, people were finding their seats, and a few thousand people finding their seats is not a quiet affair. It buzzed like a beehive in the auditorium and I was convinced that nobody was even remotely paying attention to anything we did. Applause at the end of each number was sparse, if there was any at all, and I started to wonder how on earth you broke through in this huge country.

Then the reviews started to appear, and although they were primarily about the headline act, we were singled out in every case as the band to watch. As the tour progressed our confidence grew and we returned to England just before Christmas, quietly confident that it wouldn't be too long before we were back in the USA.

Early into the new year I was sitting quietly in the little house in West Harrow when the telephone rang. A voice on the other end introduced himself.

"My name is David Moss and I am a chartered accountant with the firm of Bryce Hamner in Albermarle Street in London. We have been retained by Atlantic Records to handle your accountancy and I need to see you as soon as possible to discuss some difficulties that have arisen. Can you come in and see me today, please?"

I panicked. I was sure something had gone horribly wrong. I agreed to get up to see him that afternoon and arrived in his oak-panelled office at two thirty.

I immediately took a liking to David Moss as he put me at ease with his opening welcome.

"Come in and sit down, Rick. I hope I didn't worry you too much with my telephone call. We do have a couple of immediate problems, but if we sort them out quickly everything will be fine."

I sat in silence while he continued.

"You are probably unaware of the record situation in America as we have only just got the first royalty statements through, but it is very apparent that the *Fragile* album is selling like hot cakes. In a nutshell, you have a very successful record on your hands that is likely to reach the top ten in the album charts over there, with sales running at least into the million mark, if not two million."

I sat paralysed.

"This basically means that you are all going to have quite a serious tax problem hitting you very hard, very shortly, and I am here to make sure you use up as many benefits as you're allowed and that your personal finances are set up as advantageously as possible. Now, I've got various forms for you to fill in for the formation of your limited company."

He pushed various pieces of paper across the desk to me which I signed where he had marked them with a cross.

"Good," he said. "Now, on to the next thing I would like you to do. I want you to buy a house."

"I've got one," I said.

"Have you got a mortgage?" he inquired. "And if so, how much is it for?"

"I have a mortgage and it's for four thousand pounds."

David took his glasses off and leaned across the desk.

"You're going to have to move quite quickly, I'm afraid. I need you to go out and look for a house in the thirty thousand pound price bracket and I need you really to find one and then purchase it in the next four weeks. Now, here's my card. The moment you find something you like, just give this card to the estate agent and ask him to call me. I'll take over from there. Oh, and by the way, put your current house on the market first thing tomorrow morning."

I sat on the train going back to Harrow on the Hill station with my mind going nineteen to the dozen. I didn't even know property existed in that price bracket. After getting off the train I found some estate agents in Harrow High Street and looked in the windows to get an idea of prices. There was nothing at all for sale in the area over twenty thousand pounds. I got home and telephoned my father and told him the situation and also what had happened up at David Moss's office.

He listened patiently.

"To find property in that price range you're going to have to go out into the stockbroker belt," he said. "Try phoning some estate agents in the Gerrards Cross, Buckinghamshire, area and ask them to send you some details of property in that price range."

Two days later I found myself looking at pictures of houses beyond my wildest dreams. Five and six bedrooms with studies, breakfast rooms, en-suite bathrooms – it was all too much to take in and so Ros and I decided to take a drive out and have a look for ourselves.

On arrival in Gerrards Cross we just drove around at first, looking at the outside of some of the houses whose details they had sent us through the post. Every single one appeared to us like a mansion. Finally, we pulled up outside a house called Southgate in Fulmer Road. It looked absolutely lovely and was on the market for twenty-six thousand, five hundred pounds.

"Let's go and have a look inside," I said eagerly, and with Ros carrying Oliver, our newly born baby boy, we marched down the path and rang the doorbell.

The ring was answered by a middle-aged and very smartly dressed lady. She had obviously never seen anything quite like me before because, on seeing me on her doorstep, she visibly changed colour and appeared to look round for something to use as protection against the attack she felt sure was imminent.

"Hello," I said brightly. "Can we have a look round your house, please?"

She obviously felt that the safest thing to do would be to let this six foot four, long-haired lout, dressed in lime green PVC trousers, into her house before the neighbours saw what was happening, and so she beckoned us in.

She turned out to be the wife of an executive who worked for Callard and Bowser, the large confectionery firm. She took a shine to baby Oliver and offered to hold him whilst we had a look round.

We loved the house. It really left its mark on us. Sadly, when we took Oliver from the lady we noticed that he too had left his mark. He'd relieved himself, and his nappy had unfortunately leaked down the front of her cardigan.

"We love the house and we'd like to buy it," I said, as we stood in the hallway after a thorough look around the property.

She looked a little stunned and suggested we went and talked to the estate agent.

Ten minutes later I walked into the tiny office of Giddy and Giddy in the Gerrards Cross town centre. It was made up simply of a reception area with a glass-partitioned office at the back. The door to this office was open and I could see a very smartly dressed gentleman sitting behind a desk. He looked up from his paperwork, saw me, changed colour and getting up from behind his desk, closed the door.

The young girl behind the reception desk was much friendlier and asked how she could help us.

"I'd like to buy Southgate in Fulmer Road, please."

She walked from behind the reception area over to the glass-panelled office, knocked on the door and went in, closing the door behind her. A few minutes later she emerged with the smartly dressed gentleman behind her. He walked over to me.

"So you're interested in buying Southgate, are you?" he asked rather sarcastically, whilst looking me up and down.

"Yes, please. We've had a look round the property and we love it."

Oliver's nappy was now leaking violently, and this was not helping the already difficult atmosphere in such a confined area.

"Do you have a mortgage set up for this purchase?" The sarcasm was unbelievable, but I soldiered on.

"No, I don't, but I was told as soon as I found somewhere I liked to get the estate agent to call this man at this number."

I gave him one of David Moss's business cards.

He took it, and with an exasperated sigh turned and went into his office. Five minutes later he emerged, with a broad, welcoming smile on his face.

"Mr and Mrs Wakeman," he began. "Do come into my

office and sit down. Shirley, bring some tea and coffee in straight away, unless of course Mr Wakeman would prefer something a little stronger?"

Mr Wakeman would.

During the next ten minutes, I witnessed the finest display of grovelling that I have ever seen. I really liked David Moss, he was my kind of accountant!

We sold the house in West Harrow for eleven thousand pounds and repaid the bank as well as the mortgage. Mr Williams was delighted, as his faith in me had proved sound, and our relationship continued right up until his retirement. By early April 1972 we had moved in. One month later I bought a Rolls-Royce Silver Cloud.

My apprenticeship course completed, I was now a fully fledged rock star!

The rest of 1972 raced by. Yes recorded *Close to the Edge*, which outsold anything that Yes had ever done previously, and we had moved up to second billing as regards concerts in America, even headlining a few shows in our own right. Bill Bruford had left the band to work with Robert Frip, and Alan White had replaced him on drums.

I was also working on my first solo album for A&M Records which I was recording on the odd days that Yes weren't touring – not very many as the band was in great demand all over Europe as well as America.

In January 1973 my first solo album, *The Six Wives of Henry VIII*, was released. The reviews were dreadful. The hierarchy at A&M Records in London hated it because it was a concept album and had no vocals. They told Brian Lane, my manager, that they were going to press up twelve and a half thousand copies and hope that they could sell them somehow in order to get the money back that they had laid out on the production costs.

The record sold in excess of six million copies over the next five years alone.

That year Yes toured Japan and Australia, as well as the USA and Europe, and a live album was recorded in America

which was released as a triple album set and called *Yessongs*.
It was one of the biggest-selling albums of the decade and
Yes was now well and truly established as one of the world's
top bands.

By the end of 1973, though, cracks had started to appear
in the Yes framework.

With the exception of me, they had all become vegetarians
in a big way. I was also the only heavy drinker in the band
and so socially we grew a long way apart. I spent most of my
spare time on tour eating curries and drinking with the crew
whilst Jon, Chris, Alan and Steve went off in search of the
nearest place that sold nutburgers.

New music was always discussed during these social hours,
and because I was leading a totally different social life and
never around with the rest of the guys, I was unable to
contribute to any musical discussions as to the direction the
next album was to take. By the time I did get involved, it
was too late.

Tales for Topographic Oceans is an album that Yes
devotees either love with a passion or hate vehemently. I
come in the latter category.

True, it has some great moments, but not enough for a
double album as far as I am concerned. Nevertheless I tried
to contribute what I could throughout the recording sessions,
in spite of having to work in bizarre surroundings.

There had been long and drawn-out conversations about
where we should record the album. At the final meeting to
decide the matter once and for all, we ended up with very
much a split decision as to whether we recorded in one of the
new studios out in the countryside or stayed in town. Brian
Lane on behalf of the management, Chris and I wanted to
stay in town, whilst Alan, Steve and Jon fancied life in the
country. Town eventually won – with a compromise. The
compromise was that we had to feel we were recording
in the country. I gave up at this juncture and went round
the pub.

I was the first to arrive at Morgan Studios, which was

situated just off the Willesden High Road in north London. There were four studios in the complex as well as a restaurant and bar area, which is where I headed on my arrival. With a large Scotch in one hand and a bacon sandwich in the other, I sat down at a table, only to be joined after a couple of minutes by Monty Babson, the studio manager and joint owner.

"Morning, Rick."

"Morning, Monty," I replied through a mouthful of sandwich.

He continued the conversation with a particularly sarcastic question.

"What time are the rest of the band arriving and are they all coming from somewhere on this planet?"

"You've lost me, Monty," I said. "It's a bit early for riddles and you know I can't start communicating until I've had a least two or three large Scotches in the morning."

He stood up.

"Well, down that one quick, have two more large ones on the house, and see me outside studio three in five minutes."

Suitably lubricated with whisky paid for by Morgan Studios, I met Monty as requested.

"Your crew arrived here in vans at eight o'clock this morning," said Monty.

"Well, of course," I answered. "They've got to load all the gear in."

"The gear arrived at ten o'clock," said Monty.

"Well, what came at eight, then?" I asked. I was getting inquisitive.

"This lot," said Monty, and flung open the double doors leading to studio three.

I have to say I was lost for words. The studio looked like a farmyard. There were bales of straw scattered liberally around, on which my keyboards were precariously balanced, and white lattice fencing was built neatly around the drum kit. Other farmyard implements added to the authenticity, but pride of place went to a huge cardboard cow that stood in the middle of the studio staring at the milk churn on which the guitar amplifier stood.

"Well?" he said. "Is my studio going to look like this for the next three months? It's farcical."

"Three months is a lot of money in studio rental, Monty," I replied, with a grin on my face.

"That really is particularly nice fencing," said Monty, and walked back to his office.

Eventually everybody showed up and recording began. It was not the easiest environment to work in. My keyboards regularly needed taking apart to remove deceased insect life and ears of corn, and nobody took my comments about foot and mouth disease very seriously, either.

Earlier that year I had played keyboards on the Who's *Tommy* at a live performance with the London Symphony Orchestra at a now defunct rock venue called the Rainbow. The show was produced by the late Lou Reisner and during rehearsals I broached the subject of my plans for my second album to see if he would like to be involved. My idea was to do another concept album, but this time in a much more grandiose manner: orchestra, choir, narrator and rock band. The works, in fact. He loved the idea and I set to work immediately on putting it all together. The concept I had chosen was that of Jules Verne's *Journey to the Centre of the Earth*.

I arranged for Danny Beckerman and Will Malone, who had orchestrated *Tommy*, to work with my short score of the overall music to produce the orchestral and choir parts, whilst I concentrated on putting a band together to perform the piece, which was to be recorded live at the Royal Festival Hall the following January.

The management and record company wanted me to get as many well-known faces as possible in the band and make it a star-studded event. I disagreed, because I wanted people to remember the music and not who had played it. One

Sunday evening I solved most of this problem in one fell swoop.

There was a wonderful little pub called the Valiant Trooper in a village called Holmer Green, near to where I lived, that I used to frequent every Sunday evening and, more often than not, sit in with a bunch of local musicians who played there on a regular basis. It was jam-packed every Sunday night, and Pete the landlord had a novel way of making the most of these occasions and raising money for charity at the same time. Basically, when someone handed over money to pay for their round of drinks, Pete would drop their change into a huge barrel, which he would empty at regular intervals and with the contents buy "chairmobiles" for the disabled.

All of the musicians who played at the Valiant Trooper were very proficient, and I enjoyed the evenings all the more because the singer of the band was my great friend, Ashley Holt, who had long since left Ronnie Smith but was still living in the Buckinghamshire area.

As the last customers left at closing time and Pete locked the doors, with me, Ashley, Roger Newell the bass player and the drummer Barney James still inside, I got the drinks in and asked the lads to sit down as I had something to talk to them about that could well be of interest.

I told them that I had a gig coming up and would like them to be the core of the band, along with Mike Egan, a session guitarist I had worked with on numerous occasions when I was regularly doing sessions. I wanted to use two singers and had chosen Gary Pickford Hopkins to sing alongside Ashley. They were all really enthusiastic and "joined up" there and then.

As I left the pub at about two o'clock in the morning, Ashley shouted after me.

"By the way, Rick. Where and when's the gig?"

I turned round in the doorway.

"It's on January the eighteenth, it's at the Royal Festival Hall and we're doing a new piece I've written called *Journey to the Centre of the Earth* with the London Symphony Orchestra and the English Chamber Choir. David Measham is conducting and David Hemmings is doing the narration."

It was awfully quiet as I closed the door.

The advance I got from A&M Records came nowhere near to covering the production costs of such an epic and I used up every penny I had earned with Yes, as well as remortgaging the house up to the hilt and refinancing the Rolls-Royce, in order to raise enough money to realise my dream.

Rehearsals went well and the concert was sold out way in advance.

"Good news about the show selling out, isn't it," said Brian Lane as I sat in his office with just two weeks to go to the big day.

"That reminds me," I said, "when can I pick up some tickets for my family?"

"I'll organise that now," he said, and asked his secretary to get Harvey Goldsmith, the promoter, on the telephone.

I could only hear one half of the conversation but sensed all was not well by what I could hear this end.

"Oh dear" featured a lot, as did "I thought you automatically put tickets to one side for the artist". Eventually Brian replaced the handset.

"Harvey's sold all the tickets."

"What about some for me?" I asked, knowing full well I was on a fruitless mission here.

"He hasn't held any back, but don't panic, here's a number to call where you can get some." He handed me a piece of paper with a telephone number on it. "It's a ticket tout who's managed to get his hands on about fifty. You'll have to move fast, though, as apparently they're going like hot cakes."

I was pretty dumbfounded but took the phone that Brian was offering me and dialled the number. An extremely well-known ticket tout answered the phone. I hastily introduced myself and explained my problem.

"How many do you need?" he asked.

"Twenty, please."

"I've actually only got twenty left now, and I'm afraid the best I can let you have them for is five hundred quid. How's that sound?"

"Extortionate," I said. "That's eight times the face value of the tickets."

"I'll tell you what," said the voice on the other end of the line. "As you do seem to be on the embarrassing end of an unfortunate situation here, I'll throw in a pair of Cup Final tickets as well, for good measure. Now how's that sound?"

"Good tickets?"

"They're in the third and fourth rows directly in front of the stage."

"I mean the Cup Final tickets."

"The best."

"You've got a deal."

The concert was a tremendous success. We did two performances in the same evening and recorded the second one. Everybody who took part gave everything they'd got. Afterwards, I was the only one who was unable to make the reception, as for the first time in my life a chink had appeared in my armour and I was genuinely feeling tired and unwell.

The reviews were great and within a week I was back in Morgan Studios mixing the live tapes. I needed to get the master completed and delivered to A&M as quickly as possible, in order to get a release date whilst the concert was still fresh in everybody's mind. Within two weeks the work was completed and I delivered it to the record company. One day after its delivery, Brian called me at home.

"We have a big problem," he said. "A&M hate the record and think it stands no chance of selling. They don't want to release it."

I was devastated. Everything I owned, plus borrowed money that I didn't, was tied up in *Journey to the Centre of the Earth*. In a few weeks' time I was about to become a father for the second time, and so the financial pressures were enormous.

"They have to release it, Brian," I pleaded. "I'll go bankrupt otherwise."

"Leave it with me," said Brian. "I have an idea that might just work. Your contract is actually with A&M in America, so I am going to send a cassette off to Jerry Moss, A&M's president, in California. I've already spoken to him, and he says if he likes the music he'll override the London office's decision."

I sweated for a week before Brian called me again.

"Jerry Moss has ordered A&M here to release it. It'll be on the streets within three weeks."

I don't think I've ever been so relieved in my life.

Yes was still a fast-growing problem for me. I did not enjoy playing *Tales from Topographic Oceans* on tour and I was fast becoming a loner within the band. In Frankfurt, during the European tour, I called a band meeting and handed in my notice. It was not taken too seriously. Everybody suggested I should wait until the tour was over before making any hasty decisions and that only then should we all meet up and discuss the situation. I reluctantly agreed.

Throughout the tour, plans for the next Yes album started to take shape and, as the musical ideas were still very much in the *Tales from Topographic Oceans* style, at the end of the tour I reiterated to the band my desire to leave.

I still wasn't taken seriously and after the tour had finished I moved down to stay in a little cottage I had bought in Devon as somewhere to get away from it all, taking the family, which now included baby Adam, who had been born in March.

May 18th 1974 was a day I will never forget for as long as I live. It started with a mid-morning phone call from Brian Lane, telling me that rehearsals for the new Yes album would be starting the following week. I told him I would not be there.

"You really are leaving, then?" he sounded genuinely upset.

"Yes, Brian. In a band you have to put in as much as you take out. I can't give much to the style of music that

Yes has moved into and so for the band's sake it's best I leave."

After a pause, Brian spoke again.

"I understand what you're saying, but I think you're mad. Yes are about to earn a fortune. Some other keyboard player is now going to benefit from all the hard work that you've put in over the last three years. Why don't you swallow your pride and just do this album and the next tour, set yourself up financially and then leave?"

I told him I couldn't do that, and the conversation finished with him asking me not to make any public announcement until they had sorted out a replacement keyboard player. I agreed and said that I would do anything I could to help the new keyboard player, whoever he might be, with arrangements of the music I had been involved in on *Fragile*, *Close to the Edge* and *Tales for Topographic Oceans* for live performance purposes. I loved Yes dearly and this had been a very difficult decision to make.

Five minutes after I put the phone down it rang again. This time it was Terry O'Neil from A&M Records.

"Rick, I've got some sensational news for you. *Journey to the Centre of the Earth* has just gone to number one in the UK album charts."

May 18th 1974 was my twenty-fifth birthday.

10

Too much too soon

As soon as Yes had announced Patrick Moraz as their new
keyboard player, I announced my intention of playing *Journey
to the Centre of the Earth* at an outdoor concert at Crystal
Palace. Supporting bands included Procul Harem and Leo
Sayer and it was all set to be one amazing garden party!

I had been working hard rehearsing the band for this
performance and had also had special effects made specially
for the event. Amongst other things there were two giant
inflatable monsters, which were to rise out of the lake in
front of the stage during a piece called "The Battle" and
fight each other.

I had also been partying in the true sense of a so-called rock
star. I was drinking very heavily and smoking forty cigarettes
a day. I was never in bed much before four in the morning
and often never got to sleep at all. I was starting to put on a
lot of weight and was struggling to keep going. We were also
in the throes of moving house yet again, to a big mansion
five miles down the road at Burnham Beeches. By the time
the day of the concert at Crystal Palace came round, I was
absolutely shattered. I drove myself there in my new Ford
Mustang, went straight to the hospitality tent and drank half
a bottle of Scotch.

By the time I appeared on the stage I felt very strange. It

was not a feeling I had ever had before. My arms ached and everything I tried to do was an effort. In spite of that, the performance went well and with adrenalin obviously helping the situation the fifteen-thousand-strong crowd gave us a standing ovation at the end.

I drove home and went straight to bed. In the morning I still felt rough, but put that down to too much drink, not enough sleep and the pressure I had been under during the previous two or three months.

I had a phone interview with *Melody Maker* booked for ten o'clock that morning and a band meeting organised at eleven. I was sitting in my study in the middle of the interview when I suddenly felt desperately weak. I fell off the chair on to the floor and passed out. A few seconds later I came round, still clutching the phone. I managed to say that I would call back as I suddenly didn't feel very well, and then literally crawled up the stairs to the bedroom, where I just managed to climb on to the bed. I felt drained and disorientated. Ros came into the bedroom, took one look at me and called the doctor, who was by my bedside within ten minutes.

He examined me, gave me an injection and then went out of the room to talk to Ros before coming back in to see me.

"I've called for an ambulance," he said, in a very serious tone of voice. "I've also called ahead to the hospital, who are awaiting your arrival."

I lay there, stunned.

"But I feel fine now," I said, trying to push myself into an upright position.

"A three-hundred-year-old corpse would feel fine after what I've just injected you with. Now lie still and wait for the ambulance." The doctor left the room again and a few minutes later I heard the ambulance pull up outside the house.

Two ambulancemen appeared at my bedside with a stretcher.

"I can walk down," I said and started to get out of bed.

"You won't," they said, and expertly manoeuvred me on to the stretcher before transporting me downstairs, through the front door and up the path towards the ambulance, where I passed the band coming the other way for the band meeting.

"Won't be long," I shouted to them. "Just got to pop down to the hospital. I'll be back in an hour."

I was discharged from Wexham Park Hospital four and a half weeks later.

On my arrival at the hospital, I was put on to a trolley and wheeled through a never-ending maze of corridors while I chatted away to a couple of nurses who were accompanying me on my guided tour. Finally we turned a corner and headed towards two large doors. I looked at the writing above the doors and froze in mid-speech as they wheeled me past the sign that read "Cardiac Arrest Unit".

During the next ten minutes I was wired up to everything except the light socket and had enough blood removed to start my own blood bank. A lady in a white coat came into the room and sat down beside the bed.

"My name's Dr Speed," she said, "and I'm just going through some precautionary measures after reading this report from your doctor and speaking to him on the telephone. You have had all the classic symptoms of a coronary, but at your age that's highly unlikely, and so as soon as we've looked at the results of your tests I think we'll have you back home by teatime."

Much relieved by the last part of her news, I lay back and relaxed.

One hour later she returned. She looked very serious as she sat down beside me.

"You're going to have to stay in for some time, I'm afraid," she began. "The results show that something has definitely occurred and we're going to have to do a lot more tests. I also want Dr Towers, who is a very eminent consultant from Harefield Hospital, to look at you."

With that, she turned on her heel and walked out. I was

taken to the heart wing, which was sectioned off into areas each containing four beds, and after being given a hospital nightie to put on was told to get into bed and await further instructions.

I said my first prayer for nearly five years.

Looking back, I suppose that that prayer was more of a desperate cry for help than anything else. I can quite vividly recall pleading with God that there was so much more that I wanted to do with my life. Whilst deep down inside I was well aware that the position I now found myself in was entirely of my own making, I felt that surely He must have a solution somewhere. He would listen to me. He would hear my cry. My situation was very much tinged with the old familiar story. When everything else has failed, give God a call.

The next few weeks were a nightmare. It culminated just before I was discharged with my being told that perhaps I should give up touring and just compose music for a living, which would be less of a strain. I thought about the situation long and hard and decided that there was no way I could give up playing live. Music was my life and there was so much more I wanted to do. I would take my chances. I had been told that this attack had been a very serious warning to me that there was only so much abuse a body could take, and it was only my age that would perhaps help me to a full recovery. I was also told to cut down both my drinking and my smoking, which they felt had been very much contributory factors to what had happened.

Whilst in hospital, I mentally composed my next solo album. It was to be based on the myths and legends of King Arthur and the Knights of the Round Table. In many respects, the album related as much to my life as it did to King Arthur's, as I honestly wondered at one stage if it would be the last record I would ever make.

One unpublicised visitor during that dreadful period whilst I lay in my hospital bed was Jon Anderson. Up until the writing of this book I have never mentioned his visit to anybody, and he and I have only ever mentioned it to each other once since, but it was a meeting that was to cement our friendship, which has lasted until this present day.

"You have a visitor," the nurse said gently, waking me from an afternoon sleep.

I opened my eyes and there by my bedside stood Jon. His face wore an expression of genuine concern as he sat down on the chair by the side of my bed and spoke to me.

"I've been very worried, Rick, that not only did you make the wrong decision in leaving the band, but that it has also brought about the situation of you being here in this hospital. Why don't you change your mind and come back to the band? I know how passionate you feel about the music and what you don't like at the moment, but the best way to change things is from within. You can't change a situation if you're not part of it. It's not too late, Rick, come back."

I gave him the wrong answer. My heart said yes but my pride said no. He gave me a hug and walked out of my musical life for the next two years.

The next few months were hectic. I toured America, Japan and Australia with *Journey to the Centre of the Earth* and then went into the studio to record *The Myths and Legends of King Arthur and the Knights of the Round Table*. After regular fortnightly check-ups at Harefield Hospital, they decided that I had made a complete recovery and need not see them any more. To celebrate, I increased my alcohol intake back to its pre-Wexham Park level and moved from cigarettes to cigars.

During the recording of *King Arthur* at Morgan Studios I began to realise that the band was getting a bit stale and was in need of change. The most significant move came with the arrival of Tony Fernandez on drums; he and Alan White are still the two finest drummers I have ever had the pleasure of working with.

The album was another epic with orchestra and choir, and I decided to perform it live at Wembley Empire Pool. The pre-production meeting took place in Brian Lane's office with Harvey Goldsmith. Both Brian and Harvey wanted me to do the concert at the Royal Albert Hall.

"You can't do it at Wembley, anyway," said Harvey, "because the only dates available are just before they need the ice rink, which means the whole of the middle section will be frozen over."

"We'll do it on ice, then," I said.

And we did.

It was an extravaganza in every sense of the world. The stage was built in the middle of the ice and was constructed to look like a giant castle. Champion ice skaters, whom I had shipped in from all over the world, skated round us depicting the various Arthurian legends. On stage was a symphony orchestra, two choirs, a narrator and a seven-piece rock band. We played three sell-out nights and the audiences loved it.

The press hated it.

The whole thing had cost an absolute fortune and, because it was way before the days of sponsorship, I had to pay for everything myself. The culmination of all this was that in spite of having already sold nearly ten million records around the world, I was virtually broke.

Later that year I composed the music for my first movie, *Lisztomania*, which was directed by Ken Russell. It starred Roger Daltrey as Liszt, Paul Nicholas as Wagner and Ringo Starr as the Pope! I even had a cameo part in the film, playing Thor. To this day I have never really understood what part Thor played in the life of Liszt. Having said that, Ken had Wagner looking like Adolf Hitler and the Pope arriving on a fairground roller-coaster, so I suppose my part was pretty normal by those standards.

That year I also ended up in South America. I was the first major artist to appear down there. It was staggering. I had no idea before I arrived in Brazil that I had sold more records there than the Beatles, but twenty-five thousand people waving and cheering at the airport in Rio de Janeiro gave me a good clue!

We performed with the Brazilian Symphony Orchestra and Choir, who were absolutely brilliant. We played *Journey* and *Arthur* on alternate nights to capacity audiences of thirty-five thousand people at each performance. Ronnie Biggs, one of the Great Train Robbers, came to every show. I remember asking him if he missed England. He just turned and looked out over Copacabana Beach, and smiled.

Halfway through the series of performances I was taken to meet the president. He sat behind a huge desk surrounded by about ten men wearing dark glasses. He spoke no English and so a linguist had been brought in to translate.

After the welcoming handshakes, the president spoke to me in Portuguese and the linguist translated into English.

"The president is very pleased to welcome you to his country and hopes you are having a nice stay."

"I'm having an absolute wonderful time," I told him, and after the translation had been made the president beamed and spoke again.

"The president says that unfortunately, for security reasons, he will not be able to attend any of the performances," (presidents in South America tended to leave office mainly through lead poisoning which usually came in the form of bullets) "but his children are looking forward to seeing both *Journey to the Centre of the Earth* and *King Arthur* on Thursday evening," came the translation.

"Could you mention to the president," I said, trying to be helpful, "that we are only playing *Journey*, on Thursday evening. On Friday we'll be doing *King Arthur* and *Journey* again on the Saturday."

After the translator had put this back into Portuguese I noticed a distinct expression change on the president's face, but it returned to a smile as he spoke again.

"The president says that his children are really looking forward to hearing both *Journey to the Centre of the Earth* and *King Arthur* on Thursday evening." The translator was now sweating profusely. "He also asks if you have had your visas renewed yet, as they have to be reissued every week."

"Very sorry," I said, smiling back at the president. "Total misunderstanding of the situation on my part. I forgot that this Thursday, and this Thursday only, we have decided to play both *Journey to the Centre of the Earth* and *King Arthur* at the evening performance. We'll also throw in most of *The Six Wives of Henry VIII* as well."

After this had been translated he beamed even more than before. The atmosphere relaxed and we shook hands as I left. Three months later somebody shot him.

It was during that tour that I put together my musical plan for the epic to end all epics. Basing it on the unknown, I had given it the title *No Earthly Connection*.

I still had fast-growing financial pressures which I kept alleviating by remortgaging the house. The problem was that in spite of the fact that my epic productions had all been very successful musically, they had drained me financially. I found myself in Brian Lanes' office once more.

"No more epics," he simply said. "The record company don't want any more and you just can't afford to do any more. The decision the record company have come to is that you produce an album with just the band. People have had enough of big productions, anyway."

I was very upset, but with no money in the bank had no bargaining power. I adapted *No Earthly Connection* for the band and added Martin Shields on trumpet and Reg Brooks on trombone to the line-up. I decided to give the band a name; in fact it was Brian Lane who came up with the idea of the English Rock Ensemble. We set off for the studios in France and began recording in January 1976.

Despite patchy reviews, the album sold in excess of three million and we embarked on a world tour. Although business was pretty good, it was blatantly obvious from the word go that this production was considerably watered down from past efforts and attendances were well down. My audience, like me, wanted extravagance. I couldn't give it to them.

Throughout the European leg of the tour I kept returning to London to produce the music for a film of the 1976 Winter

Olympics which had been held at Innsbruck. The film was called *White Rock* and the album bore the same name. I was given my head as regards the style of music and chose out-and-out synthesised rock with a few sweet melodies thrown in where appropriate. The reviews of both music and film were excellent, as both areas had been really innovative for that time. The camera-work was nothing short of sensational and revolutionised the way winter sports would be filmed from then on. Similarly, from that moment, every sporting film seemed to have rock music attached to it.

As the tour came to an end late in the summer, Brian Lane and the accountant David Moss called me to a crisis meeting. Crippling taxes and interest charges on the huge bank loans had taken their toll beyond repair. I would have to fold up the English Rock Ensemble and put my house up for sale.

I spent the next month closing down everything to do with the band. Everybody was very sad. Not just because they were now all out of a job, but because it really was a great band with great camaraderie, and that was something that was lacking in so many bands at the time.

Two days before Guy Fawkes' night, the phone rang in my now up-for-sale house.

"Alex Scott here, Rick."

Alex was Brian Lane's assistant.

"I'm in Switzerland at the moment with Yes. I've got Jon here and he wants to talk to you."

Jon came on the line.

"Listen, Rick, we're just about to start recording a new album here at Mountain Studios. The music's right up your street. I'm going to send you a cassette to listen to a few of the demos, and when you've heard it call me back and we'll talk about the situation."

The tape came containing three songs and I loved all three. It was musically much more like the Yes I knew and loved, and I got straight back on the phone to Jon, bubbling with enthusiasm. I agreed to fly to Switzerland for further discussions and two days later was being driven from Geneva airport along the lakeside to Montreux.

Brian Lane suggested to me that I performed on the album as a kind of session musician, in other words, receive a flat fee. This, he said, would also help me to solve some of my financial difficulties. The rest of Yes were in agreement and so after returning home to collect some warm clothes, I went back to Switzerland on November 11th to start recording.

After just a few days I was really enjoying myself, as once again I found myself being able to contribute to the music. I felt part of the band, but in reality was only there as a guest. At the end of the week, Claude Nobs, the head of Warner Brothers in Europe, invited us all up to his house for a party. I found myself getting extremely drunk with Chris Squire, who eventually turned to me and said, "You're going to cost us a fortune, d'you know that?"

"No," I slurred back. "How come?"

"Well," said Chris, "it'll be at least three months before we've finished this album which means you'll pick up a small fortune in session fees, and then we'll be going out touring and you'll have to come with us as you'll be the only person who'll know how to play your parts, and that'll cost us another small fortune. It's silly, really. I think you should rejoin the band properly. After all, it's just like you're back in anyway."

"Absolutely," I said, and waved goodbye to a small fortune.

Three days later the *Melody Maker* arrived in the studio from England. On the front cover was a picture of the five of us sitting in the control room of Mountain Studios. This time the headline above the picture read, "Wakeman Rejoins Yes."

Very imaginative, these journalists.

11

There's no place like home

Recording the new album with Yes and living away from home had put a great strain on my marriage. Ros didn't particularly like travelling and was not keen on leaving the family pets with friends and coming to Switzerland to visit me. Also the boys, Oliver and Adam, were at nursery school and it made it difficult for us to find either the time or place to be a family.

To add to the difficulties, the accountants had told me that the only way I could get myself out of the current financial difficulties was to do a tax year out of the country. They suggested I stay in Switzerland as I would be recording there until March anyway.

Ros and I discussed the possibilities of the family moving to Switzerland to join me, but for a variety of reasons it never happened and I moved into a flat in Blonay, a few miles outside Montreux.

It would be unfair to say that we then just grew apart, as it was I who became very much the separatist. Whilst not entirely to blame for the marital collapse, I admit I made little effort to salvage the situation as it stood and the marriage fell apart.

I found myself going out with the studio secretary, Danielle Corminbouef, and by early 1977 we were living together in my flat. Ros filed for divorce and my financial situation worsened as all the marital possessions were sold to pay for the settlement. I now owned nothing. Danielle and I were eventually married in January 1980 in the West Indies.

The Yes album was finally finished in mid 1977 and called *Going For The One*. It is in my view one of Yes's best and contains the band's only British hit single, "Wondrous Stories", which got to number seven later that year, and also the piece of music which to me still epitomises everything that Yes music should stand for, "Awaken".

Once again we were off touring around the world and I was starting to get back on my feet again. I was now renting a house up in the mountains and had bought myself a Range Rover for getting around in the snow. Danielle was expecting a baby early in the new year and, apart from the fact that my parents and family now disowned me, life was great.

I hardly spoke to my father or mother for two years. I let our relationship fester badly. I could only ever see my side of any situation. Eventually, my parents agreed to come to Switzerland to stay for a week and an uneasy truce was forged. By this time I had bought a large house in Les Monts de Corsier and, with David Bowie and Charlie Chaplin as near neighbours, had well and truly settled in.

I plunged headfirst into both work and play. I produced three more solo albums in Mountain Studios, *Criminal Record*, *Rhapsodies* and *Rock 'n' Roll Prophet* as well as travelling to England to record the *Tormato* album with Yes at Rak Studios. My drinking was now out of all proportion; although I didn't realise it at the time, I had become an alcoholic.

Yes continued to tour, but the popularity was waning as the public demanded new ideas and young faces. They found it in the unlikely form of punk and new wave. It was now late in 1979 and Yes had just finished a tour of America which had been fraught with problems. A new album and fresh approach were desperately needed. Jon and I wrote half a dozen songs together and presented them to the band. They were not received favourably.

Nevertheless, a studio in Paris was booked for the months of November and December for the initial work on the new album. To try and keep some sort of control, Roy Thomas Baker was brought in as producer.

Day after day, Jon and I would sit in the studio trying to get some enthusiasm out of everybody, but invariably to no avail. Eventually the situation sorted itself out, thanks to Alan White, who went off roller-skating one afternoon and broke his leg in the process – not actually too helpful when you're a drummer, especially one who's recording a new album at the time.

A band meeting was called and it was decided to try and carry on for a few days to see if Alan could play with his leg in plaster, but the band's heart wasn't in the recording. One evening Jon and I sat in a little café opposite the studio, drinking Calvados after Calvados, trying to come up with a solution to the situation we found ourselves in. Finally, Jon looked at me and spoke with tears in his eyes.

"This isn't Yes you know. This isn't how it's meant to be. We're meant to make music, Yes music. I can't do this any more. It's time for me to leave."

I couldn't imagine a Yes without Jon (and still can't) and so I found myself saying, "I think you're right. If you're out then I'm out, too."

We went back to the studio, found Brian Lane and told him what we were going to do. Quite sensibly he suggested we all calm down, go home for Christmas and then meet up early in the new year to discuss the situation.

He got some of it right. We all did calm down and we all did go to our respective homes for Christmas, but we never met in the new year to discuss the situation. Jon and I stuck by our decisions, and quit.

Yes signed up Trevor Horn and Geoff Downes, who were then known as the Buggles, to replace Jon and me, recorded an album called *Drama*, and went off on an American tour, at the same time neglecting to tell the paying public over there that Jon and I had left the band, which did not go down very well.

I put the English Rock Ensemble back together again and we went off touring around Europe. The climate was bad for progressive rock, though, and popularity for my style of music was at rock bottom. Eventually, after a few months, I had to fold the band up again.

Brian tried to put a supergroup together consisting of Carl Palmer on drums, John Wetton on bass and myself on keyboards and actually had a deal signed, sealed and delivered with Geffin Records in America. We also had Trevor Rabin lined up as the guitarist that we wanted, but because the record company were happy to sign us without hearing us play or even talk about the style of music we wanted to do, I refused to sign the contract on a matter of principle. By doing this I basically sealed my financial fate, and things went downhill fast.

I started a small record label called Moon Records but with little or no success. I ran the company from a small office opposite the casino in Montreux. My one and only employee was Danielle's sister, Jackie, who spoke four languages fluently and was engaged to one of the Swiss artists on the label.

It was a cold November day, November 25th to be exact, and the day had been pretty uneventful. At five o'clock I'd had enough.

"Come on, Jackie, let's go down the White Horse and have a few drinks. There's nothing going to happen here today so we might as well shut up shop."

We closed up and wandered down to the local pub where everybody seemed to converge at all hours of the day. At six o'clock, Jackie said that she was just going to pop back to the office and see if there were any messages on the Ansafone; if not she was going straight on home.

Fifteen minutes later she was back.

"I think you'd better come back to the office," she said.

"There's a really strange message from your father on the Ansafone that I think you ought to listen to."

We walked back to the office. After rewinding the tape, I pressed the play button.

"Richard," said my father's voice. "I need to speak to you urgently. I'll wait here in my office until six thirty for you to call me back. It's very important, so make sure you call me."

I looked at my watch. It was half-past six. I tried calling but got no reply. Then I realised that we were an hour ahead of the UK and so he would be on his way home.

I decided against telephoning home in case it worried my mother. I was very puzzled, though, as my father and I rarely called each other these days. I was always too busy to find the time to speak to anybody unless they were in the pub. I went back to the White Horse, had a few more drinks and eventually went home.

I opened the post before going to bed. I remember every letter I opened was a bill. One of them was from the telephone company, informing me that through non-payment of the account my phone would be cut off at nine thirty the following morning. I had another drink and went to bed.

I awoke to the sound of the telephone ringing. I looked at the clock. It was nine o'clock. I staggered out of bed into the hallway where the telephone was on a small desk. I slumped into a chair and picked up the receiver.

"Richard."

The voice seemed vaguely familiar but I couldn't place it exactly.

"This is Jack Gilmore."

Now I knew who the voice belonged to. He was my parents' next-door neighbour. I was puzzled. Why on earth would he phone me? And how did he get hold of my telephone number?

I heard him take a deep breath before speaking.

"Richard, I have some bad news for you. I think you

had better come home immediately. Your father died this morning on his way to work."

I replaced the receiver and sat stunned for a full five minutes.

And then I cried.

His voice on the Ansafone continues to haunt me to this very day and has left me with a quite genuine fear of answering the telephone. My father was just ten days away from his retirement. In fact, on the very morning that he died, he had been discussing with my mother the arrangements for their upcoming holiday and so I know that there was nothing sinister, such as a premonition of death, as regards his uncharacteristic call to me in Switzerland.

The funeral was a numbing experience. I felt desperately low. I loved my father so much and had never really told him. He had been so inspirational in my life and I had never thanked him. In the last few years he had needed me and I hadn't been there.

I said my second prayer in ten years.

I kept saying sorry. Sorry to my father, sorry to my mother and sorry to God. I asked all three to forgive me.

My finances were now in a complete mess and bankruptcy was a distinct possibility. David Moss introduced me to Tony MacArthur at M.A.M., a huge entertainment set-up. They were very powerful and handled Tom Jones, Shirley Bassey and Gilbert O'Sullivan amongst many other notable entertainers. David hoped that Tony MacArthur could salvage something from my seemingly impossible situation.

Tony began the new year by getting me a new record deal with Charisma Records, and I teamed up with Tim Rice to write my first epic for nearly six years. It was based on George Orwell's *1984*.

The budget was big enough for me to use a full choir and orchestra as well as a band, and I also managed to persuade some very talented vocalists to come on board as guests: Jon Anderson, Steve Harley and Chaka Khan.

The record came out to good reviews and reached twenty-two in the British album charts. Tim and I planned to put it on as a musical but the lawyers acting for the George Orwell estate put the blocks on our plans, and eventually we had to shelve the project. To add insult to injury, Charisma lost their licensing agreement in America, and so the album ended up with limited releases around the world. However, I still put yet another new band together and a tour was organised in order to promote the album.

We rehearsed in Switzerland and then went off on tour around Europe and South America. I returned from South America to find my marriage on the rocks. Actually, to be more precise, I found my suitcase on the step and Danielle in Belgium with a nineteen-year-old catering student.

I picked up the suitcase and flew to London where I slept wherever I could. Some nights I slept on park benches before getting moved on by the police. Even this had its amusing side, as most of the police who moved me on knew who I was but had no idea of the mess I was in. A typical scenario would start with me being shaken by one of the boys in blue out on his beat.

"Come on, Rick. Been out clubbing again? Well at least you've got the common sense not to drive. I suggest you find a cab quick and get off home before the wife finds out you're not back."

We would then all have a good chuckle, I would thank him profusely, walk off in the other direction and when he was out of sight return to the park bench until morning.

When the tour started I at least had a hotel room to go to every night, and when I did reach it I was invariably drunk as a skunk. My life had, in reality, collapsed and my career was fast following suit.

Whilst up at M.A.M. finalising the tour in 1981, I had been approached by a guy called Martin Pursey who was an in-house publisher. He had come across a record that I had released earlier in the year in France with a Swiss girl singer. The record was called *Folies Bergère* and was, if the truth be known, pretty dreadful. However, he had really taken a fancy to it and asked if I could supply him with the backing track so that he could put an English vocal on it. I said that it would be no problem and that I still had the original lyrics in English if he wanted them. We agreed to produce this new version as a joint venture, and I left him to it.

Over the next week in the studio he tried at least half a dozen female vocalists. After I had heard every one, we decided that either none of them could sing or the song was rubbish. He said he had one more vocalist to try and after that we'd give up. On listening to contestant number seven, I came to the conclusion that she was undoubtedly the best so far and that we would go with her. I also came to the conclusion that the song was definitely rubbish.

The singer's name was Nina Carter.

Halfway through the tour in November, I got a message from Martin that a photographer was coming to the show in Oxford to take a picture for *Music Week*. It was to do with the release of *Folies Bergère* and Nina Carter would be coming down to the theatre for the photograph with me.

By the day of the Oxford show I had forgotten all about *Music Week* and the photographer, and after the sound check had gone straight over to the nearest pub.

At about six thirty, a man carrying three tons of camera equipment came into the pub and after looking round and spotting me, shouted, "Ah, Rick. There you are. We've been waiting for you over at the theatre."

We've been waiting?

Then I noticed the young lady next to him, wearing this enormous wide-brimmed hat. I instantly recognised her as Nina Carter, and then I remembered.

"Sorry," was all I could manage.

"Not to worry," he said. "We'll do the picture in here. Good atmosphere. Much better than the normal head shots. Right, just stand over by the bar. Put your arm round her, Rick. That's it, smile."

He fired off three or four shots and then joined us for

a drink. He said he couldn't stay for the show but Nina expressed an interest in watching the first half-hour before she had to go on to another appointment. I asked Paul, our tour manager, to organise a ticket for her and, realising the time, got the band together and went back over to the theatre to do the show.

The tour came to an end a few days later and I managed to find myself a cheap flat in Queensway, West London. Another message came via Martin that Kent Gavin at the *Daily Mirror* wanted to do a picture of Nina and me for publication sometime before Christmas as part of the launch of the record. A date was fixed and two days later I found myself on my first "professional" photo shoot!

After the session had finished, we sat and had coffee. I had already fallen hook, line and sinker for Nina, but didn't ask her out simply because I had been told that she was engaged to a wealthy printer in Nottingham and was about to get married. I decided that in these circumstances a poverty-stricken piano player stood little chance in the contest, especially as the engagement ring on the fourth finger of her left hand would probably have fetched enough on the diamond market to have solved most of my financial problems in one fell swoop.

Back at M.A.M., though, Martin painted a slightly different picture. He told me that there was a strong rumour going about that she was not entirely happy in her current relationship, but as it was only hearsay he couldn't confirm the story. I decided to take a cautious route on the subject.

Making arrangements through Martin at the record company, I invited Nina out for a half-business, half-social evening in order to discuss possible promotion for the record and also to chew over any future musical plans that she had. I worked on the principle that if she thought I was trying it on she would decline the invitation and that would be the end of it all, but to my considerable amazement I received an acceptance. Two days later we met in Morton's, a club in Berkeley Square, before going off to see Michael Crawford in *Barnum* at the London Palladium.

Over an Indian meal after the show, I gleaned as much information as I possibly could about her life both past and present. There was quite a lot that I already knew. I knew that she was one of the first page-three girls and had gone on to become one of Europe's top models, appearing on the cover of virtually every magazine there was, including *Vogue*. She'd probably even been in *Exchange and Mart*! I also knew that in the mid-seventies she had formed a band called Blonde on Blonde with her best friend, Jilly Johnson, who was also a model. They had actually had quite a lot of success, especially in Japan and the Far East. What I did learn from the evening, though, was that Nina's life had had more than its fair share of problems and in many ways ran parallel with everything that had happened to me.

After getting thrown out of the restaurant at three o'clock in the morning because they wanted to close, we ended up back at my flat where, when Nina had finished telling me about her life, I started telling her about mine. We were still talking at nine o'clock in the morning when she left for a photo shoot in town.

"I'm going to Switzerland tomorrow to see my little boy for Christmas," I said in passing to her as she was leaving.

"Here's my telephone number," she said. "Call me on Christmas Day."

At five o'clock on December 25th, I crunched my way through the snow on my way to the telephone kiosk at the bottom of the road in Blonay, where my ex-wife still had an apartment and where she had come for a few days over Christmas with Benjamin, our three-year-old boy, to see her family. I dialled Nina's number and after a few rings she answered.

We talked until I had run out of money and arranged to meet as soon as I got back. She finished the conversation by telling me that she was about to officially break off her engagement. I walked back up the hill deep in thought.

My mother was unaware that my marriage had folded up and also that I was now going out with a model whose reputation as a rebel was almost as bad as mine. The death of my father had hit her really hard and sadly had not really brought us any closer together. Eventually, it seemed that the whole world knew Nina and I were going out together except for my mother, so I telephoned her with the news before somebody else did. She was not impressed. Nina had already warned me that she probably wouldn't be overwhelmed at hearing that another marriage had gone down the tubes and probably wouldn't be too excited at my new relationship either. To put it mildly, Nina was spot on.

I listened at the other end of the phone whilst, between the tears, my mother laid into me with a vengeance. She told me that as I'd got it wrong so many times before, I was bound to get it all wrong again. Why did I never listen to anybody? My father had forecast this all along. "If he could see the mess you're in now he'd turn in his grave."

This one-way conversation continued in a similar vein for at least five minutes. Nina had also forecast this and had warned me not to get involved in an argument, so only when the torrent of abuse had finished did I say my prearranged piece.

"I know what you're saying, Mum, and I don't disagree with a lot of what you've said, but what I actually called to talk to you about is Benjamin. He's coming over to England to see me next week for a couple of days and I thought it would be nice if you came out to the airport and saw him for half an hour before he flies back home. Nina will be with me, so you can meet her at the same time."

The torrent immediately restarted at the point it had finished a minute or so earlier. Exasperated, I managed to scream down the phone that if she didn't turn up, it may well be the last time she saw either me or Benjamin and that it was her decision. I slammed the phone down.

"How did it go?" Nina asked me later that day.

"As expected," was the best I could come up with.

That week I moved in with Nina at her little terraced house in Godalming, Surrey. That week, Benjamin came to stay, and at the end of that week, when we took Benjamin to the airport, my mother came to see him off and meet Nina. From that day on, my mother and Nina have been as close to one another as anyone could possibly imagine and my mother and I became inseparable.

Nina's next self-set task was to reunite me properly with my eldest two boys by organising regular visits and weekend trips. There is little doubt that Nina was solely responsible for uniting the Wakeman family.

Our major problem was still financial, though. Nina's finances were in almost as bad a shape as mine and my second album for Charisma, *Cost of Living*, did nothing to improve the situation.

Nina had made it very clear that she never ever wanted to get married. She had been married once and it had been a disaster. She pointed out that, having two failed marriages behind me, I was no advert for marital bliss either. We did, however, discuss children. Nina loved my boys but wanted children of her own before she got too old. During the early part of 1982 she miscarried twice. After numerous medical tests, we discovered that Nina had a serious problem in relation to carrying a child throughout the full term of pregnancy, and so as soon as we discovered in July that she was expecting another baby, the doctor put her under constant medical supervision.

Nina's house was very tiny and totally unsuitable to bring a young baby into, so we decided to move. We knew that this wasn't going to be easy as, in a nutshell, neither of us had any money, but Nina had bought her house at the right time and it had now doubled in value, producing an equity of nearly thirty thousand pounds. Armed with this information and details of a near-derelict eleven-bedroomed house in Camberley that could be bought for eighty-two thousand, five hundred pounds, I went to see David Moss.

David had remained a good friend throughout all my troubles and was keen to try and help me back on my feet. He knew of only one building society that would even consider loaning to a couple like Nina and me, but said he would do the best he could to try and get us an offer.

By late October we had an offer from the London Building Society, subject to all the usual searches and surveys. Things seemed to be picking up and with Nina well into her pregnancy and seemingly doing well, early November saw us travelling by train to Edinburgh, where we were going to stay for a couple of days whilst I promoted my new album *Rock 'n' Roll Prophet* by doing interviews at Radio Forth and personal appearances at record shops.

On our arrival late in the afternoon we checked into the St James Hotel and Nina said she felt very tired. I had an appointment at the radio station and so I left Nina in bed asleep whilst I went off to do the interview.

The interview was going very smoothly and I was enjoying myself. Halfway through the recording, I noticed out of the corner of my eye that someone had come into the control room and was talking anxiously to the engineer. I sensed something was wrong and my suspicions were confirmed when they stopped the interview by asking me to come into the control room. There I was given the news that Nina had been found haemorrhaging in the hotel room and had been rushed to Simpson's Hospital.

I was at the hospital within minutes. A nurse sat me down and spoke to me before I was allowed to see Nina. She explained that Nina had lost a lot of blood and that they thought it doubtful that they could save the baby. They wanted to keep her in overnight, though, as they had sent for a special piece of scanning equipment which was currently in Glasgow but would arrive in the morning and would enable them to give a proper appraisal of the situation.

I saw Nina and tried my best to offer her some encouragement, but she was very distraught and was convinced that she had lost the baby. I went back to the hotel and drank a vast amount of whisky.

The following morning I arrived at the hospital only to be ushered into a small room and told to wait. I was convinced I was about to receive confirmation of what we already suspected, and so I sat preparing myself for what I was sure was about to happen. A young doctor came into the room, closed the door behind him and sat down.

"Well, I'm very pleased to be able to tell you that the baby is still alive, Mr Wakeman," was his opening line, and I just sat there speechless, both relief and excitement churning around inside me.

"There are one or two quite serious problems, though," he continued, "which you must be made aware of. Your wife has been told the situation and now I'm going to explain it to you."

I sat in silence and listened to what he had to say.

"Nina has a very complicated form of placenta praevia," he began. "In layman's terms, that means the womb is blocked by the placenta, which in turn means that there is nowhere for the baby to come out when it's ready to be born. This will mean a caesarean birth, which under normal circumstances is not a problem, but in Nina's case it is. We will not be able to monitor the baby's progress as we would really like and we will have to choose very carefully the time when we will perform the birth by caesarean section. Lastly, Nina cannot be moved. It is far too dangerous for her, and I have spoken to her doctor back in Godalming, who agrees. Now, how does that affect you?"

"No problem," I lied, "I can easily make the necessary arrangements to move up here for a couple of weeks."

"I don't think you've fully grasped the situation," he said quietly. "Nina is going to be here at least until the end of February."

As I walked down the corridor towards the maternity wing, I weighed up the situation.

We were in Scotland with Nina bedridden for the next three and a half months.

We were in the process of moving house and had no money in the bank.

I had little or no work, prospects were grim and M.A.M. were about to fold up, following a court case over monies owed to Gilbert O'Sullivan.

In a nutshell, I was now managerless, penniless and homeless.

I arrived at Nina's bedside.

"Don't worry," I said. "I've got everything completely under control. I'll be popping home tomorrow to pick up the car and Lamb-chop and bringing them back up here." (Lamb-chop was the unfortunate name that Nina had given to her border collie.) "I've got one or two places in mind as to where we'll stay," (the back seat of the car was actually the best option I had, but I thought it best not to worry her at that particular moment) "and I'll bring all my recording work and writing up here." (I knew this wouldn't be a problem as I didn't have any.) I left Nina in a positive frame of mind and the following day took the train back home.

I drove Choppy back with me (I refused to call the dog Lamb-chop) and arrived back in Edinburgh in the early hours of the morning. The hotel had offered me a room that night for nothing, but after that I was out on my own.

It was Richard Findlay, the head of Radio Forth, who came to my rescue. Initially he called me into his office and showed me a comprehensive list of flats that were available for short-term rent in the Edinburgh area. I politely scoured the proffered pages, throwing in the occasional "Now that looks nice" and "Is that in a nice area?" before handing the list back to him.

"Nothing suitable?" he queried, still obviously eager to help.

"Nothing really in my price range," I replied.

"How much can you actually afford to spend? I'm sure we can find something."

I decided not to waste any more of his time.

"To be brutally honest, Richard, I'm broke. I'm also meant to be moving house in two months' time, which at this present moment looks highly unlikely as the mortgage has been prepared in joint names and I hardly see the building society accepting that arrangement with Nina stuck in hospital. There's also another complication. I found out this morning that Nina's house in Godalming has been sold, so when she does eventually come out of hospital with the baby we could all be living in the back of my old car."

Richard looked genuinely concerned.

"Does Nina know about all this?" he asked.

"Oh look," I said. "There's a herd of pink and yellow striped piggy-wiggies flying by your window."

"Point taken," he said, and I left his office to go and collect my belongings from the hotel and then check out.

On my arrival at the hotel, I was given a message at the reception asking me to call back at Radio Forth and see Richard Findlay, and so a few minutes later I found myself back in his office.

"I've got an idea," he said. "I live out at Aberlady in a large house that has an old annexe attached to it. It's got no heating, although there is an open fireplace, and there's not much furniture, but it's completely self-contained and you're welcome to it. I don't want any money, I'd just like to help if I can."

I could have kissed him. I moved in straight away, and from a local second-hand junk shop bought a mattress which I balanced on some old beer crates, some cheap bedding, a second-hand television with an indoor aerial and some saucepans to cook with. There was an old cooker already fitted which I got going after a thorough clean and a good kicking. There was electric light in all the rooms, and I loved the place. It was one of the happiest periods of my life. I walked the dog on the beach every morning before going to see Nina in hospital, then drank vast quantities of Famous Grouse whisky in the afternoon before going to see her again in the evening.

Barclays Bank, who now had the dubious honour of being the latest institution to bank with me, were actually very understanding about the whole situation, and through David Moss arranged a small overdraft facility enabling me to draw a few pounds out every week in order to eat, drink and run the car. In retrospect I didn't do much eating and I walked nearly everywhere.

Potential disaster came in the form of a telephone call from Willie Robertson, the insurance broker who was dealing with my mortgage. Because of the fact that Nina was now unable to have a medical in order to get the life assurance needed for the mortgage, the insurance company required me to have another, more substantial medical examination before issuing the building society with a new policy to cover the shortfall. An appointment had been made for me with a Dr McPherson in the outpatients' department of the hospital where Nina was currently housed.

I panicked. I was not in good shape. I had not been eating properly and was still drinking heavily. I was not overweight but certainly out of condition. I had stopped smoking three years earlier, which was a plus, but overall I felt the chances of me passing this medical were not good. On top of everything there had also been my little stay at Wexham Park Hospital, which would just about wreck any chances I had of getting the medical all-clear. For the two days before the appointment I just drank water.

I arrived at the hospital and waited for my name to be called. Eventually my turn came and I was ushered into a small cubicle which was simply curtained off from lots of other adjoining cubicles. After a few moments a middle-aged man walked through the curtaining and slumped into a chair. He did not look at all well.

"I'm Dr McPherson," he said.

I was in two minds whether to call for a nurse, but before

I had time to reach any decision on the matter he looked up and spoke again.

"It was the golf club dinner last night. Wonderful game, golf, you know. Do you play it yourself?"

I couldn't have told you which end of the club to hold, let alone play it. I knew nothing about the game at all. However, I felt that any points that I could score with the doctor could only help me in my quest for medical clearance, and therefore I looked straight into his bloodshot eyes and spoke with the obvious passion of one who lives for nothing but the noble Royal and Ancient game.

"Of course I do," I said. "Finest game in the world."

The bond was struck.

We went through the insurance form in the usual way, and eventually he came to the question on alcohol consumption.

"Do you like a drink?" he asked.

"Occasionally," I ventured back.

"What's your tipple?"

"Scotch."

"With what?"

"Nothing, just Scotch on its own."

"Good man," he said, and picking up his pen wrote down after the question on alcohol consumption "Drinks in moderation."

When we came to the question of heart trouble he became quite serious and gave me an ECG test and a pretty thorough going-over. To complete the medical, he had to bring in a nurse to take some blood samples from me, as after he had made at least three abortive attempts to find a vein in my arm, his hands were shaking so much that he quite simply gave up.

The medical over, he asked me what it was all in aid of. I told him the whole story from start to finish and eventually thanked him and left to visit Nina in the maternity wing.

One week later I got a telephone call from Willie Robertson regarding my life assurance.

"I've just had a telephone call from the insurance company who have in turn just received your medical report."

I drew a deep breath, fully expecting the worst.

"Rick, I know you're a drinker, and that you haven't exactly looked after yourself over the years, but this report defies all logic. Apparently you are one of the fittest men in the United Kingdom at this present moment, and according to this report you really should be spearheading our gymnastics team at the next Olympics. I don't know how you've done it, but you've had your policy accepted, which in turn means you've got your mortgage. Give my love to Nina." And with that, he rang off.

Jemma Keira Wakeman was born by caesarean section at Simpson's Hospital in Edinburgh on February 21st 1983. Two weeks later, I drove Nina and Jemma to our new home in Camberley on which I had exchanged contracts one week earlier.

12

Third time lucky

We settled in nicely as a family in our new home and I worked hard at trying to get some income flowing. It was not proving easy, as my kind of music was still about as popular as a contraceptive machine in the Vatican and I no longer had a record contract. I spent a short time with Yellow Balloon Management, who looked after Bobby Davro, but their experience in the rock field was limited, and so eventually moved on and at the end of the year teamed up with Brian Adams and Eddie Hardin, who were two guys who ran a studio near my home in Sunningdale.

I signed a small record deal with Eddie Kassner and his son David, who, apart from running a large publishing house also owned President Records.

I formed a new band in order to produce my first album for President, and with a line-up that included Tony Fernandez on drums and Chas Cronk on bass, we produced the LP *Silent Nights*. The record was well received and the single *Glory Boys* was a minor hit.

Things were starting to look up. The record company were happy, the management were happy, I was happy, and thought Nina was happy. I arrived home one evening, and after dinner she said she wanted to have a little chat.

Clutching a large brandy, I sat down in the lounge and waited for her to begin her "little chat".

"I want to get married."

"Pardon?"

"I don't want to live like this, I want to get married."

"But I thought you said you never wanted to even contemplate marriage again as long as you lived?"

"I've changed my mind, and if you loved me and wanted to marry me then you would have pushed your divorce through by now and asked me to marry you."

There endeth the first rollicking.

It was early 1984, and there I was, quietly sitting in the lounge with my glass of brandy, when suddenly the nice "little chat" seemed to be aiming right at the proverbial jugular.

It happened completely without warning and confirmed all my previous suspicions as regards women's logic.

I'll do my best to explain.

Without making matters too complicated, both Nina and I had been married before. (To reiterate, I had had a couple of previous attempts and Nina had just had the one.) Subsequently our joint marital record was not exactly one that offered particularly great odds as to success in the area of future wedded bliss.

Having said all that, and setting the scene somewhat, it must be said that I had always wanted to marry Nina from day one. It was in fact Nina who had been the one to consistently pour cold water over my marital aspirations, with such emphatic marriage guidance statements as "Anyone who gets married these days has got to be completely stark raving mad", and "Who on earth in their right mind wants to get married anyway, it always ends in disaster".

There are of course other well-known legendary classics used constantly by divorced men and women contemplating remarriage. Here are a few examples:

"You only want to marry me for my money."

"I suppose it helps your tax situation."

"It's easier to get a joint mortgage than for either one of us on our own."

And of course the woman's classic,

"We'll have to get married as you're totally incapable of looking after yourself."

Whatever happened to love?

Anyway, whether by design or otherwise, Nina had successfully managed to steer me off the subject of marriage for nigh on three years, in fact right up until this particular moment.

Life, of course, was now about to take a distinctly different route. It was never going to be quite as simple as just phoning up the registry office and booking a day to get it over and done with, life is far too complicated for that. For starters, I was still married!

Getting my divorce finalised was not easy. In true rock and roll style, I (an Englishman) had married my second wife (who was Swiss) in the sea (in Barbados).

The paperwork needed for the divorce exceeded that of the Maastricht Treaty, and probably cost as much as well, but finally I got the decree absolutes – yes, absolutes. I needed decrees from Barbados, Switzerland and the UK! (This has often led me to wonder exactly how many times I have actually been married.) Nevertheless, Nina and I finally found ourselves sitting down to plan the wedding arrangements.

"I want to be married in a church."

I now seriously questioned her sanity.

"We've got absolutely no chance of that, so you can put that idea right out of your head now."

"Well, you used to belong to a church, give them a ring and see what they say."

I no longer had any contact with the Baptist church at South Harrow but nevertheless phoned up the local Baptist church in our area, and then the Methodist, and then the Church of England. I even contemplated the synagogue.

Each of these telephone conversations lasted less than ten seconds, so I gave up.

I then tried to explain, in as nice a way as possible, to my future wife that churches were very anti marrying people who had been married before, and as we had had no less than three previous attempts at it between us, and all three had been consummate failures, we had had it.

Woking Registry Office, here we come.

It has to be said that the lady who greeted us on our arrival at the steps of the office for the registration of births, marriages and deaths was very helpful, pleasant and efficient. She went through all the necessary paperwork with us and checked over available dates on which she could perform the ceremony. Finally, she put down her pen and looked up from her desk at us, waiting for our response.

It came from Nina.

"I'm not getting married in here. People die in here."

Nina had once again felt an inner need and compulsion to completely discard tact and subtlety in her approach to the current situation in hand.

I quietly explained that whilst it was in fact quite true that deaths were registered here in this very building, people didn't actually come into one of the offices and keel over, nor did they book a time at which to do so.

"I don't care. I'd rather just live together than say a few meaningless words in this place. My first wedding was in a registry office, and look what happened there. It's all right for you, you've been married in a church."

"And look what happened to that marriage," I replied.

I knew the moment I had uttered that last statement that I had made a mistake.

A big mistake.

Immediately the greatest weapon known to the female sex was brought into play.

Tears.

Floods of them.

"I so wanted to get it right this time." (The sobbing

continued throughout the soliloquy.) "I wanted the day to be something very special, and now there isn't going to be one."

The lady from the registry office stood up behind her desk and in a very matter-of-fact tone said, "Have you tried the United Reformed Church? They sometimes marry couples who have been divorced."

The tears and sobbing subsided to a mere torrent, and within fifteen minutes we were driving back to Camberley. I had actually seen a United Reformed Church in the town and so we decided to find it before going home.

When we arrived there we found nobody around and all the doors were locked, but we noted down the vicar's name and address from the notice-board outside and went home in order to call him on the telephone.

With no real idea of what to say any more, I dialled his number.

"Hello, Graham Long here."

Nervously I introduced myself.

"Er, hello. My name is Rick Wakeman."

From the total lack of response or apparent interest after this statement, I immediately assumed he had no idea who I was. This, I felt, could be a distinct advantage to me as my rebel-rousing days had been extremely well-documented over the years. To be in the almost unheard-of position of talking to somebody with a relatively clean sheet in my hand seemed to be something of an advantageous novelty.

"My fiancée and I would like to get married."

Not subtle, I admit, but that was all I could manage to blurt out at the time.

"Well, I think you and your fiancée had better come and see me, so that we can all sit down over a nice cup of coffee and have a serious talk about your plans and aspirations."

I felt that this was now probably the best time to come clean rather than lead him too much up the proverbial garden path and therefore waste his valuable time, and so said, in a voice that I hoped sounded full of the necessary repentance, "I have been married before."

There was a silence which seemed to last for some considerable time.

"Hello, are you still there?"

"Yes," he replied, "I did hear you, and I must say to you, before we go any further, that we at the United Reformed Church look at each case on an individual basis and only make decisions to marry couples in situations such as yours if we are a hundred per cent certain that it is right and proper for us so to do, and to gather all the necessary information in order to reach such a decision could take some considerable time."

An afternoon meeting was set up for the following Thursday. After thanking him for his time and replacing the receiver, I gave Nina the somewhat promising news.

Looking as respectable as we possibly could (I wore a tie and Nina had on a skirt that almost reached her knees), we walked up the pathway to Graham Long's house and nervously rang the bell.

The door was opened by a tall, very friendly-looking man in his mid to late thirties. He had short, slightly thinning hair. I was convinced that the first thing he noticed about me was my thick, extremely long hair.

"Come in," he said. A very welcoming smile on his face immediately put us at our ease, for a couple of minutes anyway!

We sat in his tiny office, Nina and I on two upright chairs and Graham in a chair by the side of his desk.

He broke the ice.

"Well, Rick and Nina, it's lovely to meet you and I hope that we can work something out for you, but there is a lot of work to be done before we reach that stage and so if it's all right with you I'd like to start this afternoon."

We nodded our approval. It really is amazing how your mouth totally dries up in these situations, rendering you temporarily incapable of speech.

"Now, first I really need to know as much about you as humanly possible. Your lives right up to this present moment, in fact. Nina, how about you starting the ball rolling by telling me what's happened in your life, and please don't be afraid of holding anything back."

She wasn't and she didn't.

For the next hour or so, Graham was treated to a life history that even in extremely mild terms would merit the description of colourful.

Graham, to his credit, listened without interruption, pausing only occasionally from his deep concentration to wipe the sweat from his forehead.

"And so that pretty much brings me up to why we're sitting here today," she concluded, sitting back in her chair.

I thought Graham had done remarkably well not to fall off his.

Nina looked at him and smiled. The roles were now somewhat reversed, with Graham apparently incapable of speech.

To help fill in the silence created by this temporary dumbness, Nina spoke again.

"I have to say, Graham, that if you think my life's been a little outrageous, then wait till you hear his." She looked over towards me and then back at Graham.

"I think we'd better have some coffee before listening to what Rick has to say," Graham somehow managed to blurt out as he got up and shot out of the room.

"Brilliant," I said to Nina once we were alone. "Now you've blown it completely. We've got absolutely no chance of him marrying us after what you've just told him. The Moonies wouldn't even entertain us after that little lot. Are you brain-dead or something?"

Nina leaned over towards me. "Listen to me, you stupid long-haired pillock," (she always had a wonderful way with words) "if we don't tell him the truth, then mark my words, somebody else will, so I recommend when he comes back in with the coffee that you tell him the truth from start to finish about your life. Believe you me. That's our only hope."

After what seemed an eternity, Graham returned with the coffee. He hadn't run away and I couldn't smell any trace of alcohol on his breath, so I felt we were perhaps still in with a fighting chance.

"Rick," he leaned forward in his chair. "Let's hear about you."

Well, I have to say it all got off to a very good start really. After all, my first nineteen or so years were very family- and church-orientated and I could see him visibly relaxing by the time I had reached 1968.

By 1978 I was considering calling an ambulance for him. There was no doubt, as I related my life story, that it was having a serious effect upon him, mostly that of stunned disbelief.

"That's pretty much it," I concluded.

We sat in silence for a few moments and then, very much to his credit, and without the aid of smelling-salts, alcohol or divine intervention, Graham spoke.

"This is not going to be easy," he said

(I could have told him that!)

I have to say, from a personal point of view, that if I had had to make a decision based on the stories that Nina and I had just related, then the chances of us ever getting married would have to be ranked alongside that of the Isle of Wight winning the World Cup.

Graham continued.

"How would you feel about coming to church this Sunday?" he said. "You see, I have to put your case before the elders of the church and very much feel, in the light of what you have just told me, that it would be advantageous if some of the church members got to see you both before I actually meet with them on Monday evening to discuss your case."

The request came somewhat out of the blue and we both paused whilst seemingly waiting for the other to answer.

Both Nina and I had expressed in no uncertain terms whilst

talking to Graham that we both very much believed in God. Speaking for myself, in spite of serious waywardness over the years, I had never ever doubted His existence, His ability or His presence. However, for Nina to say openly she believed in God was something new to me.

Nina broke the silence.

"Yes, we'd love to. Can we bring our daughter, Jemma? We'd very much like to organise a christening for her sometime, perhaps after we're married, or maybe you could do the lot at the same time?"

I got Nina out of the manse before any more damage could be done and, feeling strangely contented, drove home.

Oliver and Adam were staying with us that weekend and so they were dragged, it has to be said somewhat unwillingly, along with Jemma to the United Reformed Church for the Sunday family worship.

It was a strange experience for me to walk into a church after so many years. Wonderful memories of South Harrow Baptist Church came flooding back. Friends I had lost contact with, nice people, caring people. Names I had not even thought about for years, indeed had forgotten, floated through my mind. I found myself wondering what had happened to them, whether or not they were still involved with the church, or whether, like me, they had drifted away.

The United Reformed Church was incredibly friendly. Graham welcomed us at the door and we sat in a pew about halfway down the church.

The service was really enjoyable. Graham was, and still is, a very fine minister, and subsequently "performed" to packed houses. His talks were interesting and informative to both adults and children alike. Well, to those children who regularly attended the church, anyway. Jemma was too young to know what was going on and Oliver and Adam were not at all enamoured with the proceedings and behaved like most nine- to eleven-year-olds in church when they're there for pretty much the first time in their lives, bored and uninterested.

For some strange reason this niggled me. Perhaps it was that I saw myself in them at that age and what the church had meant to me way back then, and yet here I found myself in church with my family, almost like an alien.

After the service, we stayed behind for coffee and biscuits and mingled with the rest of the congregation, some of whom we vaguely knew or had seen locally in the town. Everybody seemed happy to talk to us, which made us feel very much at home. I suppose as newcomers, both as visitors to the church and newly arrived in the area, we were bound to attract attention of one sort or another, but eventually we said our goodbyes and drove home for Sunday lunch.

Graham had not mentioned our meeting or the marriage even once that morning, but that didn't concern us in any way as we'd genuinely enjoyed ourselves very much and the thought of any possible ulterior motives on Graham's part hadn't even crossed our minds.

On Monday evening the telephone rang.

I picked up the receiver.

"Graham Long here. Is that you, Rick?"

Suddenly the events of the last few days flashed before me in a kind of instant replay. I suppose the best way to describe it would be in the same way you hear of people saying how their whole lives flashed before them just before they thought they were about to die!

"Oh. Hello," I replied. "Listen, Graham, Nina and I really enjoyed Sunday. Thanks for making us so welcome."

I was rambling, desperately trying to steer the conversation away from what I felt was the real purpose of his call, the news that he was unable to marry us.

He cut my ramblings short.

"I've just finished my meeting with the elders of the church and one of the matters raised this evening was that of Nina and yourself wishing to be married before the eyes of God."

"Did you have to tell them everything we told you?" I enquired tentatively.

"Pretty much so," he replied.

I felt it was now my task to try and make it easier for him to break the news to us, however painfully bad it was. After all, we'd never have got even this far without his help and belief in us.

I spoke, already resigned to what I felt was inevitable.

"I would imagine then, Graham, that the elders are not very keen on the idea of the United Reformed Church marrying us, and in a nutshell you're calling up now to offer us your sincere condolences and wish us good luck etcetera for the future. Am I about right?"

There was a short pause, and then Graham spoke.

"Rick, I knew that if I only had your life stories as evidence to present on your behalf as to your true feelings and reasons for wanting a church wedding, then we were really dead and buried, and that's why I wanted people in our church to see you both on Sunday. I felt that if they could put real faces to the situation they were about to have thrust upon them as regards your wishing to be married in church, and also hopefully see for themselves that you both genuinely wish to start afresh and see this as a true commitment and a way to fulfil that new beginning in a right and proper way, then we might stand a chance."

He paused for breath.

"Now, how are you fixed for November the tenth?"

I really can't remember exactly what I muttered back down the telephone to Graham, except that it was full of sincere gratitude for him and what he had done for us. Finally, confirming with him that the date was fine and arranging a meeting for an evening later that week to discuss matters further, I replaced the receiver and told Nina the news.

She smiled, and I seem to recall a tear in the corner of one eye, but whatever understandably blurred recollections I may have of that actual moment, it certainly brought to the surface insurmountable proof as to the existence of the component, well known to man, that has been used to great success by the female form for centuries: that when a woman wants something badly enough, she always somehow manages to get it.

For me, the week had seen the replanting of a Christian seed somewhere within my messy life. Graham had unwittingly, or perhaps wittingly, given me a renewed faith in the Church which had been sadly lacking in my life over the previous fifteen years, ever since I'd moved away from South Harrow, in fact, shortly after being baptised.

Whilst I had never lost my faith, my feelings towards organised religion and churches in general had been extremely tarnished over the years just by my witnessing what was going on around me. Hardly a week ever seemed to go by without news of a war starting up somewhere in the world, with the blame, more often than not, attached to one fanatical religious group or another. Then, of course, those weird new religious sects were popping up all over the place, especially in America, where the rule of thumb as regards their idea of Christianity appeared to be "anything goes", and from what I read, it often did!

I was firmly convinced that in general the Church and most of the organised religious groups around the world had lost their way. To me they seemed solely concerned with structuring their own particular churches and gatherings around lifestyles that suited them, rather than those based around that of true Christianity.

All of this seemed miles away from my own interpretation of the Scriptures, but to counter-attack on behalf of those very organisations that I felt were not worthy of any true Christian's membership, could not my "not belonging" to a church or religious group have been unconsciously based around my own personal lifestyle? After all, the Church and upholding a good Christian lifestyle certainly didn't fit in with my hard-drinking, rock 'n' roll image.

Graham's faith in Nina and me had started me rethinking my Christian values. He had brought my thoughts, feelings and past before two judges – God and myself.

And both those judges didn't particularly like what they

saw. My own personal defence failed miserably to stand up to any serious self-examination, however hard I tried, but thanks to all the events of those few days, the seed had been sown for a new future and it was to grow slowly but surely from that moment on.

The wedding itself was wonderful, a true showbiz affair in every respect. I'd lost my driving licence earlier in the year through a drink-driving offence, and so a good friend had kindly supplied a fleet of Rolls-Royces for the day, with a chauffeur-driven vintage model for Nina and me to travel in. The Camberley police had shut off the roads around the church (it's a pity they didn't shut them off the day they arrested me for drunken driving) and an aeroplane flew overhead towing behind it a huge banner that read "Congratulations to Rick and Nina". Press photographers and TV cameras were everywhere and the guest list read like the proverbial *Who's Who* of the entertainment, sporting and showbiz world. A huge crowd filled the road outside the church, hoping to catch a glimpse of the bride as she arrived.

Robert Powell not only took the reading for us during the actual wedding ceremony, but also produced the now legendary "Quip Of The Day".

On arrival at the main door of the church, he was questioned by the ushers on duty as to whether he was a guest of the bride or the groom. This, as is common practice at all weddings, was to ascertain on which side of the church he was to sit.

To the stunned amazement of the ushers and other guests around him, Robert replied, "Season ticket holder!" and walked straight in.

Jilly Johnson, Nina's close friend and compatriot from her modelling days, was her maid of honour, and my drummer, Tony Fernandez, repaid the honour I had had of being best man at his wedding by returning the compliment and being my best man at mine.

The service was truly memorable in every respect. The

signing of the register was, however, somewhat confusing and took considerably longer than the time that had been officially allotted for the purpose. The main ceremony over, Graham, Nina and I, plus the witnesses, had walked over to the side of the church where the register book lay open ready for our signatures.

I signed first.

"Now you, Nina," whispered Graham.

"What name do I sign?" she whispered back.

"What do you mean?" Graham sounded nervous.

"Well," said Nina, "my maiden name is Mallet and my first name isn't Nina, it's Penelope Jane, as you know, and also my name became Trennary after my first marriage but it was changed to Carter for career purposes by some sort of deed poll."

To the best of my recollection the register book at the United Reformed church in Camberley now reads, in relation to the entry recording our marriage, under "Husband", Richard Christopher Wakeman, and under "Wife", Penelope Jane Nina Carter Mallet Trennary Wakeman!

The reception was held at Kempton Park Racecourse. At that time I had a driver who had been taken on for a year because of my enforced lack of a driving licence. He was a nice enough lad, but because of two unfortunate flaws in his make-up was nicknamed "Route Map Winfield".

The "Route Map" part was there simply because he had absolutely no sense of direction whatsoever, and he never once succeeded in getting me to where I was meant to be going without a drama along the way as regards the route he chose. The "Winfield" tag came about when he succeeded in successfully writing off my car, whilst at the same time writing off a brand, spanking new Mercedes, which just happened to be owned by the chairman of Woolworth's. Winfield was of course the name used by Woolworth's at that time for their own brand products.

As regards the wedding, Route Map Winfield's only task of the day was to lead a convoy of cars, each containing guests unfamiliar with the area, from the United Reformed Church at Camberley to Kempton Park Racecourse for the reception.

Two hours after the celebrations had actually begun, and only after somebody had kindly pointed out that half of the invited guests were actually missing, did we discover that Route Map Winfield had taken them to Sandown Park Racecourse by mistake.

(From that moment on I took taxis, trains and buses everywhere I went.)

I had organised my band to play throughout the evening, but they were soon joined by the likes of Rick Parfitt from Status Quo and John Entwhistle from the Who. Paul King from Mungo Jerry, Jess Conrad and most of the Showbiz XI football team suddenly appeared doing additional vocals and Jim Davidson took over the microphone as master of ceremonies.

It was a wild night. The place was full of television personalities such as Frank Bough, Debbie Ash, Bobby Davro, Dickie Davies, John Stapleton and his wife Lynne Faulds–Wood and most of the team from the now defunct TV-AM. The national press were there in force; ironically, the evening solved a little problem for the media, as all week long they had been searching for a young lady called Katie Rabett who had been spotted around London with Prince Andrew. The press felt sure there was some very special romance about to blossom here, especially as Katie had disappeared and apparently gone into hiding.

She had gone into hiding, but not with Prince Andrew. Katie very kindly showed up at our reception with Chris Quintin, who at the time was starring as Brian Tilsley in *Coronation Street*.

That put paid to yet another royal romance!

It all finally ground to a halt at around two o'clock in the morning, with Nina and myself the last two remaining survivors. We were both completely shattered with exhaustion, exhilaration and, it has to be said, a slight over-indulgence in the alcoholic beverage department. The vintage Rolls-Royce then completed its final task of the day by taking us to the Shepperton Moat House where we just found enough time to sort out our wedding presents and clothes, most of which had to go back to our house, before collapsing in a heap and then driving down to Salcombe Regis in Devon for our honeymoon.

Somehow we managed it, and after grabbing a couple of hours sleep set off with Nina at the wheel of a Rolls-Royce Silver Shadow, donated for the honeymoon period as a wedding present from Peter Vernon Kell, an old business acquaintance of mine.

The honeymoon was not an unqualified success. It bucketed down with rain for the first two days and on the third Jemma caught measles and was quarantined in the hotel.

Jemma was not even two years old and very much needed Mum there all the time as her "nurse". Daddy couldn't drive and so therefore was also quarantined. Unable to assist very much in the nursing capacity, Daddy became helplessly caught up in a magical honeymoon world full of nappies, spots and sleepless nights!

The hotel room was small and the rain beat constantly against the window. These two very basic elements, combined with tiredness all round, stretched our combined patience to the absolute limit. After about six days I reckon I must have just about driven Nina up the wall.

"Get out and have a game of golf," she suggested. (I had taken up the game a few months earlier and was totally addicted to it.) "It'll do you the world of good," she continued. "It's pointless us both being stuck in the hotel room day in, day out. I can't go out and leave Jemma with you, but if you go off for a few hours then I might be able to catch up on some sleep while you're gone."

"And how do I get there?" I asked. "I can't drive, or had you forgotten that?"

"Take a taxi. There must be loads of courses around this neck of the woods."

Eagerly I scoured the telephone directory and picked out a course just a few miles from where we were staying, called Bigbury Golf Club. I telephoned them, explained the situation and asked if I could play the course as a guest sometime that week.

They were extremely helpful, but explained that they had quite a busy schedule that month and that the only time that was available for visitors to play was on the following Thursday morning.

On Thursday morning it rained.

In fact it rained so hard that rivers all over south Devon were overflowing and roads were flooded for miles around.

I took a taxi to Bigbury Golf Club.

Battling against driving rain and a force nine gale, I went into the pro shop and inquired if the course was playable.

The club professional stood behind the counter and looked at me in stunned amazement.

"You want to play in this?" he said incredulously.

"Yes," I replied cheerfully.

He looked out of the window to where a veritable waterfall was gushing over the top of the first tee, pouring its way down the fairway before finally coming to rest in a small lake that one could only presume was under normal conditions the putting surface for the first hole.

"Well, the tees and greens are unplayable and most of the course is flooded, plus there's a storm going on that's got the coastguard on full alert, but I suppose if you want to hit some balls down the fairways that you can still see grass on, it's up to you."

I played all eighteen holes – well, to be exact, all eighteen fairways. I lost twenty-seven balls, an umbrella and my trolley. You needed a rowing boat to reach most of the course.

Three hours after splashing my way down the first fairway, I staggered into the changing-room and got out of my wet clothes and made myself look as respectable as possible before walking through into the clubhouse.

The clubhouse was packed. Heaving, in fact. I'd never seen a clubhouse at any golf club before that was so full at eleven thirty in the morning.

I walked up to the bar and ordered a large Scotch.

A very official-looking gentleman was sitting at the bar. He had a superb handlebar moustache and wore a blazer emblazoned with the Bigbury Golf Club insignia. I guessed, correctly as it turned out, that he was probably a relatively high-ranking official within the club.

I paid for my drink and turned towards him.

"Dreadful weather, isn't it."

"It is that," he said. "Can't remember it ever being so bad at this time of the year."

"Well," I said, "I must say you have a very flourishing club here. It's really marvellous to see so many people in the clubhouse at this time of day, especially considering that you're a fair old distance from the village."

"It's not usually this full," he replied. "It's just that word's spread that there's some pillock from London out there trying to play in this weather and they've all come up to see if they can catch a glimpse of him."

He paused for a second, looked at me closely, and with a not unfriendly smile slowly consuming his face, turned to the milling throng, pointed at me and said, "It's him!"

Jemma completed her quarantine period the day the honeymoon came to an end. We said our goodbyes and drove home.

Graham Long became a regular and very welcome visitor to our house over the next few months, and although Nina and I did not become regular attenders at the United Reformed church, the bond between Graham and us continued to grow.

One year later, Graham was to pay a visit to our home and present me with an opportunity to water the very Christian seed that he had planted during the first week of our knowing each other all those months ago.

At the time it didn't occur to me, but now I realise that everything that happened back then was part of a plan, God's plan. He was working within me and also within those around me.

This particular visit would eventually turn out to herald the beginning of yet another very important phase in my Christian self-rehabilitation, and yet it all seemed so innocent and insignificant as Graham and I chatted over an afternoon cup of tea.

13

The Gospel's trail

The new year was spent promoting *Silent Nights*. I toured the UK, America and Australia and ended up seriously in debt as the tours had been badly costed out by the management and I was left owing the shortfall. I was forced to remortgage the house and was feeling at a very low ebb. Almost the only good thing that happened that year was in September, when I gave up drinking during the Australian leg of the ill-fated tour.

I had been drinking like a fish in order to try and compensate for the disastrous tour, and finally it caught up with me. For the first time in my life I found that I couldn't handle a drink. Just two or three beers and I was drunk. One brandy and I felt quite ill. I knew there was something wrong and stopped drinking there and then and, when the tour was finally over in October, I went to see my doctor in London. He told me that it was about time I grew up and realised that I couldn't go on drinking for ever without expecting something like this to happen. He said that in his opinion my drinking days were over. I thought back over the last days of the Australian tour.

One particular morning in 1985, after being violently sick in my hotel room in Sydney, I had sat on the end of my bed and cried. I had never felt so low in my entire life. I felt ill mentally as well as physically. I realised that I had never been in control of my life since becoming a professional musician, although for years I had thought I was. Some key moments of my life appeared vividly before me: my baptism at South Harrow Baptist Church, my father's death and my marriage to Nina at the United Reformed Church. They all appeared to be shouting out to me.

Eventually a strange calmness seemed to come over the room and I found myself looking heavenward. Ill as I felt, I found myself smiling and there and then made a decision I should have made years before. The decision was to put my life back in God's hands. I asked Him there and then to forgive me for all that I had done and to give me the strength to start again. I knew it would not be easy and knew that it wouldn't happen overnight, but at least I knew I was back in safe hands and that somewhere, somehow, He would show me what I had to do in my life.

Back home in Camberley, Nina was expecting our second child, and that contributed as much as anything else to the second major decision that I made in that two-month period, which was to stop drinking, permanently. My last drink had been in Sydney, Australia, in September 1985 and I have not had one since.

Finances dictated that I needed a major record deal and in order to try and obtain one I put together the plans for a major concept album based on *The Time Machine* by H.G. Wells. Polydor loved the idea and took the project on. I began recording in a studio on a boat moored on the River Thames near Weybridge which was owned by Tony Clarke, who had produced albums for the Moody Blues and Clannad. Unfortunately the initial recording sessions did not go well and I called a halt to the proceedings to take stock of the situation. It was during that break that I received an afternoon visit from Graham Long that was ultimately to set me on the musical path which I now know was intended for me all along.

"How's the recording going?" Graham asked politely as Nina poured the tea out.

"Not very well, I'm afraid, Graham," I replied. "But I'm sure it'll all work out all right in the end. How are things with you?"

"Very good," he answered enthusiastically. "We've been left rather a large sum of money which has specific instructions attached to it – it must be used for the purposes of music within the church. This actually has come at a very good time for us as our present pipe organ is rather beyond repair and so we've ordered an Allen electronic organ from America. Do you know that particular make?"

I did and knew they were excellent. I complimented him on such a good choice.

"There is one slight problem, though," he said with a sigh. "The organ is costing a little more than the amount of money that we've been left and so we're making up the difference with a series of fund-raising activities. The organ will be installed before the middle of the year and we thought it would be nice to have an organ recital as a final fund-raiser to cover the last payment. We also wondered if you would be interested in doing the performance for us."

I felt genuinely honoured to be asked. I also felt that this was a God-given opportunity to repay some of the faith and kindness Graham had shown towards Nina and me over the previous year and a half.

"I'd love to," I said and a date was fixed there and then.

As soon as Graham left I set to work on a programme for the concert. I made a provisional list of possible pieces, which included organ works by Bach and Handel plus a few pieces that I had written for church organ myself, such as "Judas Iscariot" and "Jane Seymour". I examined the list when I had finished writing, and then tore it up.

This was a special occasion and it demanded special attention. It also demanded special music. I decided that I would write some new music based on a Christian theme. I chewed a few ideas over in my mind. The parables were a possibility; so was the story of Noah. In the end I decided it should be from the New Testament and went and got my Bible from the bookshelf. I opened it at the index page for the New Testament and found myself looking directly at the four Gospels. The decision was made. I would compose some music based on the Gospels.

I went to bed with my head buzzing about how I would go about composing the music, and woke up in the morning eager to get to work. After two hours of reading through the first few chapters of Matthew, I realised that I had taken on one almighty task. I drove into London and bought as many books as I could find on the New Testament and the Gospels in particular, came home and started making notes.

I came to the conclusion that it could not work instrumentally and so needed to be sung. I also knew that I didn't want it to be rock-orientated and so another sort of singing would be required. Ramon Ramedios immediately sprang to mind.

I had met Ramon at a charity performance at the Dominion in London and we had exchanged telephone numbers for the usual "no apparent reason". I had been a fan of his singing for years and was genuinely thrilled to meet him. During our conversation he had said that nobody ever wrote with a particular voice in mind any more, and that perhaps I should think about writing something especially for him. I'm sure he never ever expected at the time that I would take him up on his offer.

I wrote four pieces, "Welcome a Star", "Trial and Error", "The Sermon on the Mount" and "The Lord's Prayer". I then telephoned Ramon and asked if he would be interested in singing them. He asked me to send him the music and he would let me know. The manuscript, plus a cassette with the piano accompaniment on it, were duly despatched. Three days later I received a return call from Ramon who told me he genuinely loved the music and would be delighted to sing the pieces I had sent him. He asked me if they were intended for a recording or a big concert.

I realised then that I had inadvertently omitted to mention to Ramon why I had actually written the music in the first place and for what purpose. I was well aware, whilst filling him in on the details, that I was also in no position to be able to afford the considerable fees that he commanded.

I need not have worried. After listening to my explanation he offered to waive any fee, and we arranged to meet at my house on the afternoon of the day of the performance in order to rehearse. With his generosity, Ramon had breathed the very important first breath of life into *The Gospels*.

After the concert, which was a tremendous success, Nina and I took Ramon and his wife Jackie to a local restaurant for a meal. Ramon was insistent that the life of *The Gospels* shouldn't end that evening.

"It needs to be recorded," he said.

"There's more than one reason why it can't be recorded," I explained. "For starters, the four pieces aren't long enough in total to make up the length for an album or CD."

"Write some more then," said Ramon simply.

"I also don't have any money to pay for studio time," came reason number two.

"Record now, pay later," came answer number two.

We laughed, but as I thanked Ramon for his generosity and watched him drive off, I began to think that he might just have the right idea after all.

For one thing I had some studio time on the boat that was paid for. Admittedly the time was meant for the *Time Machine* project, but that was going nowhere and *The Gospels* excited me. As regards more music, I knew it was bursting to be written. Over the next few weeks I read all four Gospels from start to finish, making notes and cross-referencing wherever relevant, and by the time I walked on to the boat to start recording, I had enough material for a double album.

I had also coerced the Midland Bank into loaning me ten thousand pounds towards the cost of recording, which meant that I didn't have to "steal" from the *Time Machine* budget after all.

I needed a narrator, and the narrator I wanted was Robert Powell. Robert and I had worked together on my *Cost of Living* album on which he had narrated Gray's "Elegy in a Country Churchyard." I broached the subject during a game of golf at Moor Park Golf Club, and the deal was struck after Robert holed a twenty-five-foot putt on the eighteenth and I missed from about three inches.

Funny game, golf.

About a week later, I got a telephone call from Eton College, asking me to take a "music assembly". I agreed and whilst I was there made friends with Ralph Alwood, the head of music and choirmaster of the Eton College Chapel Choir. By the time I drove home the Eton College Chapel Choir were on the team.

The recording was fraught with technical problems that were more inhibitive than anything else. The studio on board the boat had only eight tracks; by the time Ramon and Robert had recorded their parts and we had added the choir, there was little room for orchestration from the keyboards, which meant severe limitations as regards the arrangements and choice of sounds. Nevertheless the recording was finally completed, and a deal was struck with Stylus Records to produce the double album and to sell it as a teledisc – in other words, advertise it on TV and sell it in large stores such as Woolworth's.

Sadly, not everybody at Stylus Records liked the idea of having a Christian record on board and, after showing a commercial for two days on Harlech Television, dropped the record and showed no more interest in it. Both the Christian and secular press had shown little interest either, and so I now expected *The Gospels* to disappear quietly into oblivion. I was to be proven very wrong.

From out of the blue I received a telephone call from an agent I had worked with many years before, Rod Weinberg. He asked me if *The Gospels* could be performed "live" as Central Television were genuinely interested in filming a performance at Winchester Cathedral. I said that I really didn't know if it could be done, but arranged to meet Rod to discuss the matter further.

After our meeting I decided that I had to take the bull by the horns and somehow put on a live performance. I knew it had to be in an impressive venue if I was to convince Central Television it could be done on a grand scale and so I chose the Royal Albert Hall. I couldn't find a promoter who would take the financial risk of putting it on and so the Midland Bank overdraft grew to cover the cost.

The concert threw up more problems than I had ever had to contend with in my entire life.

First of all I found that most of my keyboards had been stolen from their storage place after the ill-fated world tour the previous year. Luckily KORG came to my rescue and supplied with me with everything I needed. The problems didn't end there, though. On the day of the concert I discovered that the choir would be unavailable to rehearse and would arrive literally only a few minutes before we were due on stage.

I was also informed that Robert Powell had been filming in South America and on his arrival back in England had been taken ill and given a course of very strong pain-killing drugs. However, he would be arriving at the Royal Albert Hall about half an hour before the performance began. Robert actually arrived about one hour before we were due to begin; unfortunately, due to the strength of the medication he had been given, he was unaware of who he was, where he was and why he was where he was unaware he was.

I could have cried.

Ramon gave me a hug and told me it would all be fine. I sincerely hoped it would be as I knew that Bill Ward from Central Television had already taken his seat in the auditorium.

The choir finally arrived and I held a hasty meeting with Ramon, Robert and Ralph Alwood, the choirmaster. It was not an easy meeting. Robert was on another planet and

Ralph was unaware of the order of any of the pieces. I decided to try and simplify things as much as I could.

"Ralph, I'll turn and look at you just before your choir entries and Robert, I'll look at you and nod my head every time you have to say one of the narratives. They're all numbered, so you can't go wrong."

"Naïve" is the only word I can think of that adequately describes the four words at the end of the last paragraph.

The audience were the most amazing mixed bag of people you could ever wish for. There were Hell's Angels who obviously were expecting a rock concert, large numbers in old Wakeman tee-shirts who were obviously expecting an old-Wakeman-type show and coach parties from various churches who I'm sure expected to hear rock Gospel music. They say you can't please everyone all the time, but looking out at the audience I felt I would be struggling to please anyone any of the time!

We started with a piece called "The Baptism" and as the first few bars went by I started to relax. I looked round at Ramon and saw that he too was looking relaxed. I looked over to where Robert was and saw that he was very relaxed. So relaxed, in fact, that he was asleep.

I panicked.

At the precise moment I panicked, Robert opened his eyes and looked across at me. I gave him a little nod, as if to say, "It's all going jolly well, just hang in there." Robert read the situation somewhat differently, though. He read my little nod as, "There's my first nod, here comes my first narrative," and it did.

I went into a blind panic and looked around for help. I looked at Ralph and he obliged by bringing the choir in. I looked at Ramon, who threw me an invisible lifebelt by just appearing to the audience as if everything was going perfectly according to plan. I followed suit, and somehow by the end of the piece we were all back together again. As the final chord died away, I looked heavenward and whispered a sort of "request prayer". "Listen God, this is for You, You know, and so any help You can give us would be much appreciated."

Under all the circumstances the rest of the performance went pretty well, although any euphoria I had was instantly quashed the moment I arrived back in the dressing-room, where I learned that Bill Ward had gone straight home immediately after the performance had finished.

The Gospels had now cost twenty thousand pounds of borrowed money and I saw no way of paying it back.

Back in May, Nina had presented me with a little baby boy whom we named Oscar. With the apparent failure of *The Gospels*, I decided that perhaps the time had come to quit music and find some other way of supporting my family. Nina would have none of it.

I had resigned myself to the fact that *The Gospels* had reached the end of its natural road, but Ramon was still convinced that the life of *The Gospels* was in fact only just beginning, and continually telephoned to tell me so.

Three days after the Albert Hall concert, I received a phone call from Rod Weinberg. He told me that he had just heard from Bill Ward who had apologised profusely to him for not being able to stay at the end of the concert; he'd had to rush off to a late business meeting. He had, however, decided not to go ahead with the idea of a performance at Winchester Cathedral. My heart sank a little, but not too much, as I genuinely felt in more ways than one that we had already achieved the impossible.

"Ah well, that's life," I said.

"I haven't finished yet," said Rod. "Bill enjoyed the concert and loved the music, and now wants to film it at Caesarea in Israel with Robert Powell, Ramon and the Eton College Chapel Choir plus the Haifa Symphony Orchestra."

I was totally lost for words.

"There's just one problem," Rod concluded. "Because the project is going to be very expensive for even Central Television, they are going to need to do a buy-out of all the necessary television and video rights from you. How do you feel about that?"

I said that was fine. I was just so thrilled at the news.

"Just out of interest," I said to Rod before putting the phone down, "do you happen to know how much I get for these rights?"

"I know the exact figure," he said. "Twenty thousand pounds."

14

The end of the beginning

Israel was a wonderful experience, both spiritually and musically. I was genuinely beginning to feel that spiritually I was being led in this very special direction, but I also somehow knew that the journey along this unique road was not going to be an easy one. Musically I was unhappy with quite a large portion of *The Gospels* music which mainly stemmed from inhibitions during the recording. I knew one day I would have to do a complete rewrite before I would be content.

On my return to England I found that there had been a change at the top at Polydor and the new hierarchy were only interested in young bands and were now very single-orientated. In a nutshell, they didn't want *The Time Machine* or me. The album was eventually finished in a studio near London without an orchestra, choir or lavish ice show. President Records eventually released it, but I had lost interest in the project by the time it hit the shops.

My record sales and royalties were not bringing in enough money to cover my expenditure or pay off crippling tax bills, and so I put yet another new band together and started doing one night stands around the theatres in order to try and boost the level of income. The advances I was being offered to make records failed to cover even production costs and I realised that the only way I would be able to continue a career in recording would be to have my own studio. By the middle of 1987 I realised that Nina and I could no longer afford to keep the house in Camberley and so it was put up for sale.

We looked at much smaller houses around the area and soon realised that in order to find something acceptable, and in a price bracket we could afford, we would have to move further out into the country. Many fruitless weekends were spent searching for a suitable property and we started to despair.

Then, out of the blue, we found ourselves on the Isle of Man.

I had accepted an offer to play in a pro-celebrity golf tournament on the island and Nina had had a private word with Paul Gaskell, the organiser, and arranged for us to stay over after the tournament for a few days, as she felt I was in need of a break. I was under extreme pressure from the tax authorities, which in turn was putting a great strain on any work I was trying to do.

We arrived on the island and were met by Paul Gaskell, who took us to the hotel. I had no idea that Nina had arranged for us to stay over for the rest of the week and ranted and raved that I just couldn't spare the time when I found out. Nina was adamant that I needed a break, and a break I was going to have. During that week I fell in love with the Isle of Man and by the end of the year we had purchased a house just outside Douglas, the main town on the island.

Our last Christmas in Camberley was very much a family affair. Nobody seemed to approve of our going to the Isle of Man, but Nina and I genuinely felt that we were both being led there and so would let nothing change our decision.

On March 22nd 1988, the move was completed and we have lived on the island ever since.

Close by the property was a small coach-house which was hastily converted into a studio, and almost immediately film work started coming in. I could now compete financially in areas such as film and television, as I no longer had to budget for huge studio costs within any fees I quoted. I formed a small record label in order to release my own product, and we were able to keep ourselves very much on an even keel.

Soon after moving in we were visited by Malcolm Convery, the minister at our village church, and we started attending the occasional service along with other friends that we made in the village.

Then, out of the blue, towards the end of 1988, I received a telephone call from Brian Lane. We hadn't spoken for nearly eight years so I knew it wasn't a social call.

"I've just had Jon Anderson in my office," he said, "and he's pretty disillusioned with things at the moment."

Jon had rejoined Yes in the mid-eighties in order to be part of their very successful *90125* album. He had stayed with the band which had then produced another album called *Big Generator*. Yes had toured both albums and were, as far as I knew, going along nicely. Not so according to Brian.

"Jon feels that Yes is trying to become too much of a pop band and he wants to return to what he calls making new music again. Does that make sense, Rick?"

In a strange way it did, and I told him so.

Brian carried on.

"Jon wants to put the original *Fragile* band back together again, make a record and then tour. What's your initial reaction?"

"Count me in," was all I needed to say.

I flew to London and met up with Jon. We had a great meeting and discussed the ideas that he had. I sensed that there could be something very musical about to blossom and I wanted to be part of it. As usual, Brian Lane was one step ahead and had already secured a recording deal with Clive Davis at Arista Records. Literally a few days later, Jon and I were on a plane to New York to sign the contracts.

After preliminary work was completed, which we had done in a château just outside Paris, we set off for Montserrat in the West Indies to record the first – and only – Anderson,

Bruford, Wakeman and Howe album in George Martin's famous Air Studios.

Chris Squire was the only person missing from the line-up as he was still very much involved with Yes, who, it has to be said, were not overwhelmed when they heard about the new A.B.W.H. set-up.

Tony Levin was brought in on bass and very quickly the album took shape. I was delighted with the way the recordings were going and was also enjoying the island. There was a nine-hole golf course near by, and I spent many a happy morning there with an assortment of borrowed clubs and balls.

Montserrat was also littered with churches and I was determined to go to a service on at least one of the Sundays that I was there and when I was not needed in the studio. My opportunity came after just two weeks.

We were considering using a small choir on one track and overheard somebody mention that the local Pentecostal church had just the choir that we were looking for. I mentioned that I had intended going to a service whilst on the island, so I could check out the choir at the same time. Jon said that he really fancied coming along, too, and so everything was organised for the very next Sunday.

When the day finally arrived Pete Smith, from Brian Lane's office, made it clear that he didn't want Jon and me going to the service on our own, and decided that we should be accompanied by him and one of the larger members of the road crew. I remember thinking at the time that it was probably the first time that anyone had ever turned up for a church service with a bouncer.

I think Pete Smith's decision was based around the usual management opinion that all rock musicians are incapable of doing anything at all without managerial guidance. I would, however, like to take this opportunity to point out that after considerable experience in the music industry I am of the opinion that the exact opposite is in fact the case.

The weekends were pretty laid back. Very little work

was done in the studio as it interfered with our Sunday cricket match against the locals. Eventually the time came to drive up to the church and I was really looking forward to going there.

"Has somebody mentioned to the Pentecostal church that we're coming to the service this evening?" I asked Pete Smith.

"Yes, you did, didn't you?" came the questioned reply.

"Why me?"

"Well, I naturally thought, as it was your idea, that you would have contacted them and sorted everything out," said Pete, in a very managerial fashion.

"Managerial duties," said Jon. "It's management's job to organise, but they never do."

"Of course we do," came a voice for the defence and the argument continued right until we had parked the car outside the church and taken our seats a few rows from the back.

It was fabulous. The congregation was ninety per cent women dressed in bright wild dresses and wearing huge wide-brimmed hats. Up by the pulpit was a band consisting of an old boy on a Hammond organ, an even older bass player and drummer and a guitarist who was probably born before the instrument was even invented.

But then they started to play.

Boy, could they play! They rocked the house down and within seconds the whole place was singing and dancing in the aisles as well as the pews. I couldn't stop smiling. They had two preachers, a husband and wife team, who were brilliant and took the service together. It was turning out just like the services you see in the movies. People were shouting "Praise the Lord" and "I repent" all over the place. I loved it.

Halfway through the service the lady preacher held up her hands asking for silence. You could hear a pin drop.

"Brothers and sisters," she began, "we have in our midst this evening four friends who are strangers to our church. I want you all to give them a big welcome."

As one, the entire congregation turned towards us and

shouted welcomes. Those near by hugged us, kissed us and shook our hands. Eventually order was restored and the service continued "normally" until its conclusion half an hour later.

I was euphoric as we drove home.

"Wonderful. Brilliant. Amazing."

"Shut up, Rick," said Pete. "You're driving me potty."

"What you don't realise, Pete," I said poignantly, "is that tonight was very special. Didn't you find it amazing that out of a congregation of at least three hundred people they spotted that we were strangers in their midst and singled us out for a special welcome?"

"Nothing amazing about that," said Pete.

"And why not?"

"Because we were the only four white guys in the building."

I had to chuckle.

The album was finished and in general received good reviews from the media. We had, however, unintentionally stirred up a bit of a hornets' nest amongst the Yes faithful, and bitter arguments broke out amongst them as to what was true Yes music. Amazingly, the argument is still going on today!

We toured all over America, Canada, Japan and Europe to wild receptions and great reviews. It was weird playing Yes material that we had actually written and even weirder not being allowed to call the band Yes, but that didn't worry me too much and I thoroughly enjoyed the direction that the music was taking.

Whilst on the American leg of the tour I met up with my old friend Dan Wooding, the very first journalist to have ever written about me way back in 1969 for the *Middlesex County Times*. We had stayed in touch over the years and Dan had now moved to California where all his work was Christian-orientated. Over a cup of coffee he told me all about his plans to start an organisation called ASSIST, through which he intended to link up churches and

Christians all over the world, especially those in Russia and the rest of Eastern Europe. In turn I told him of the way that God was working in my life, albeit at a much slower pace! Dan asked me if I would like to get involved with ASSIST and I happily agreed to help where I could.

The tour over, we returned to Europe and within a few weeks began recording the second album in Mirabelle Studios in the south of France. There were a few disagreements over the material to be used for the album, and as recording progressed it became evident that the album had become a bit of a compromise which was unacceptable to me. Before the situation even approached boiling point, Brian Lane called a meeting at which he told us that a merger between the current Yes in California and A.B.W.H. was distinctly on the cards; if it could be pulled together somehow then it would solve a lot of problems for everybody.

Yes were also in the middle of recording an album, and the general plan was to merge the two products, produce one album and call it *Union*. (When I heard the finished product I renamed it "Onion" as it made me cry every time I played it.)

More time was obviously needed to enable the albums to be merged successfully, but time was something that I didn't have. I had a solo tour contractually booked and so was very limited to the amount of extra work that I could put in on the project. The end result was, as far as I was concerned, an unmitigated disaster and the worst piece of Yes product ever released to the general public.

The tour, however, was a totally different kettle of fish.

I arrived in Florida for the rehearsals, full of excitement and expectation. I sensed in a strange way that such a tour would only ever happen once, as there were too many personality clashes waiting in the wings for a head-on musical fight, so I had already decided that I was not going to get involved in Yes politics but just thoroughly enjoy performing the music – and that is exactly what I did.

It was wonderful playing with Chris Squire and Alan White

again, and Trevor Rabin and I also struck up a tremendous
relationship. The tour lasted nearly a year and virtually went
round the world, with the last performances taking place in
Tokyo early in 1992.

Contractual difficulties then meant that my time back
with Yes had come to an end yet again, and I went off
touring with my own band around America, doing small
clubs, and in South America, playing huge arenas. The things
seemed to be on the up until the Inland Revenue shattered
everything by issuing a High Court writ for nearly seventy
thousand pounds, which they claimed was interest charges
and penalties for tax that I had paid over the previous six
years by instalments. I was devastated. I could not lay my
hands on seven hundred pounds, let alone seventy thousand.
I had just three weeks in which to come up with the money.
After all the hard work I had put in over the last few
years in trying to get my life going again, I bluntly turned
down the advice given to me by my accountant to declare
myself bankrupt and lose everything I had worked for, and
made two very positive decisions: number one, to sack the
accountant, and number two, to come up with the money
from somewhere. I dealt with the first issue and Nina solved
the second.

Both took phone calls to achieve their aims. Mine just
took one but Nina's took several. It all culminated, with
help from Brian Lane's office and Yes's accountants, in my
signing away all publishing income from everything I had
ever written in order to raise the money for the taxman. I
was now right back at the starting blocks again. Twenty-two
years' work had just vanished in the three seconds it had
taken to sign my name.

Strangely enough I didn't feel it was the end of the world.
True, I now had to start building a new musical catalogue
from scratch, which was unlikely ever to be worth a fraction
of the twenty-two years' worth of compositions that I no
longer owned, but I felt that I had been given a clean sheet
of paper on which to map out my new life and it was up to

me to make sure that everything that appeared on that piece of paper was led by my fast-growing Christianity. Nina and I now belonged to Broadway Baptist Church on the Isle of Man and our involvement in the church grew accordingly. Our Sunday worship as a family is of paramount importance to us as growing Christians. We feel that just having a faith is not enough any more and that the only way forward is actual participation in that faith. At Broadway Baptist, Jesus is the only celebrity and that's how it should be.

I produced two albums, *In the Beginning* and *Prayers*, with the proceeds going to ASSIST, and formed Hope Records to look after my Christian recordings. *Prayers* in particular was another important stepping-stone for me. Prayer manifests itself to so many people in so many different ways, whether personal or shared, whispered or shouted. Using the gift that God gave me, I put my prayers to music. In mid 1994 I travelled to California and did a series of piano recitals for Dan and his charity. I did seven performances. The first had an attendance of two hundred. By the time I did the seventh and final performance, word had spread and the attendance was seven and a half thousand. I knew then that I was at last on the right road.

I came home and rewrote *The Gospels* from start to finish. I also added a new piece to the work, entitled "The Cross".

For years people have asked me what, in my opinion, is the best piece of music I have ever written and I have always been unable to answer them. With the arrival of "The Cross" I can now give them an answer.

For years I had been journeying along the roller-coaster ride of life, which continually brought me back to my starting place. Finally I had found the roller-coaster ride of Christianity, which is never-ending.

Although it is impossible to summarise my life in a few meagre sentences, two years ago I discovered a prayer attributed to an unknown Confederate soldier. Whoever that soldier may have been, we are kindred spirits.

I asked for strength that I might achieve;
I was made weak that I might learn humbly to obey.

I asked for health that I might do greater things;
I was given infirmity that I might do better things.

I asked for riches that I might be happy;
I was given poverty that I might be wise.

I asked for power that I might have the praise of men;
I was given weakness that I might feel the need of God.

I asked for all things that I might enjoy life;
I was given life that I might enjoy all things.

I got nothing that I had asked for;
But everything I had hoped for.

Almost despite myself my unspoken prayers were answered;
I am, among all men, most richly blessed.